GNU Libidn Reference Manual

A catalogue record for this book is available from the Hong Kong Public Libraries.

Published in Hong Kong by Samurai Media Limited.

Email: info@samuraimedia.org

ISBN 978-988-8381-69-2

Background Cover Image by https://www.flickr.com/people/webtreatsetc/

Table of Contents

1 Introduction

GNU Libidn is a fully documented implementation of the Stringprep, Punycode and IDNA specifications. Libidn's purpose is to encode and decode internationalized domain name strings. There are native C, C# and Java libraries.

The C library contains a generic Stringprep implementation. Profiles for Nameprep, iSCSI, SASL, XMPP and Kerberos V5 are included. Punycode and ASCII Compatible Encoding (ACE) via IDNA are supported. A mechanism to define Top-Level Domain (TLD) specific validation tables, and to compare strings against those tables, is included. Default tables for some TLDs are also included.

The Stringprep API consists of two main functions, one for converting data from the system's native representation into UTF-8, and one function to perform the Stringprep processing. Adding a new Stringprep profile for your application within the API is straight-forward. The Punycode API consists of one encoding function and one decoding function. The IDNA API consists of the ToASCII and ToUnicode functions, as well as an high-level interface for converting entire domain names to and from the ACE encoded form. The TLD API consists of one set of functions to extract the TLD name from a domain string, one set of functions to locate the proper TLD table to use based on the TLD name, and core functions to validate a string against a TLD table, and some utility wrappers to perform all the steps in one call.

The library is used by, e.g., GNU SASL and Shishi to process user names and passwords. Libidn can be built into GNU Libc to enable a new system-wide getaddrinfo flag for IDN processing.

Libidn is developed for the GNU/Linux system, but runs on over 20 Unix platforms (including Solaris, IRIX, AIX, and Tru64) and Windows. The library is written in C and (parts of) the API is also accessible from C++, Emacs Lisp, Python and Java. A native Java and C# port is included.

Also included is a command line tool, several self tests, code examples, and more.

1.1 Getting Started

This manual documents the library programming interface. All functions and data types provided by the library are explained. Included are also examples, and documentation for the command line tool `idn` that provide a quick interface to the library. The Emacs Lisp bindings for the library is also discussed.

The reader is assumed to possess basic familiarity with internationalization concepts and network programming in C or C++.

This manual can be used in several ways. If read from the beginning to the end, it gives a good introduction into the library and how it can be used in an application. Forward references are included where necessary. Later on, the manual can be used as a reference manual to get just the information needed about any particular interface of the library. Experienced programmers might want to start looking at the examples at the end of the manual (see Chapter 9 [Examples], page 38), and then only read up those parts of the interface which are unclear.

1.2 Features

This library might have a couple of advantages over other libraries doing a similar job.

It's Free Software

> Anybody can use, modify, and redistribute it under the terms of a free software license.

It's thread-safe

> No global state is kept in the library. All functions are re-entrant.

It's portable

> The code is intended to be written in pure ANSI C89. It has been tested on many Unix like operating systems, and Windows.

It's modularized

> The library is composed of several modules, and the only interaction between modules is through each modules' public API. If you only need one piece of functionality, it is possible to take the files you need and incorporate them into your own project.

It's not bloated

> The design of the library is based on the smallest API necessary to implement the basic functionality. It has been carefully extended with a small number of high-level wrappers to make it comfortable to use the library. However, it does not implement additional functionality just for the sake of completeness.

It's documented

> Sadly, not all software comes with documentation these days. This one does.

1.3 Library Overview

The following illustration show the components that make up Libidn, and how your application relates to the library. In the illustration, various components are shown as boxes. You see the generic StringPrep component, the various StringPrep profiles including Nameprep, the Punycode component, the IDNA component, and the TLD component. The arrows indicate aggregation, e.g., IDNA uses Punycode and Nameprep, and in turn Nameprep uses the generic StringPrep interface. The interfaces to all components are available for applications, no component within the library is hidden from the application.

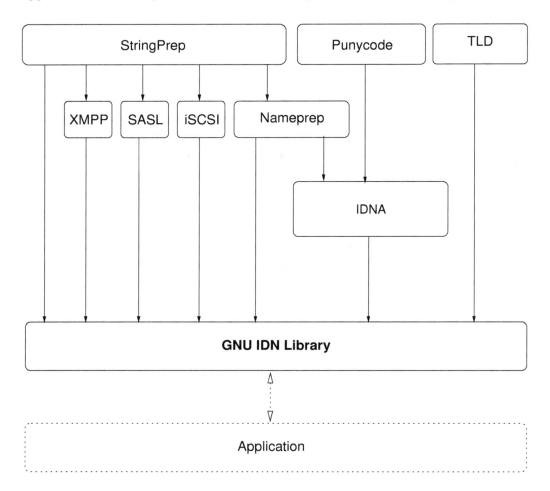

1.4 Supported Platforms

Libidn has at some point in time been tested on the following platforms. Build reports for each platforms and Libidn version is available at http://autobuild.josefsson.org/libidn/.

1. Debian GNU/Linux 3.0 (Woody)

   GCC 2.95.4 and GNU Make. This is the main development platform. `alphaev67-unknown-linux-gnu`, `alphaev6-unknown-linux-gnu`, `arm-unknown-linux-gnu`, `armv4l-unknown-linux-gnu`, `hppa-unknown-linux-gnu`, `hppa64-unknown-linux-gnu`, `i686-pc-linux-gnu`, `ia64-unknown-linux-gnu`, `m68k-unknown-linux-gnu`, `mips-unknown-linux-gnu`, `mipsel-unknown-linux-gnu`, `powerpc-unknown-linux-gnu`, `s390-ibm-linux-gnu`, `sparc-unknown-linux-gnu`, `sparc64-unknown-linux-gnu`.

2. Debian GNU/Linux 2.1

   GCC 2.95.1 and GNU Make. `armv4l-unknown-linux-gnu`.

3. Tru64 UNIX

   Tru64 UNIX C compiler and Tru64 Make. `alphaev67-dec-osf5.1`, `alphaev68-dec-osf5.1`.

4. SuSE Linux 7.1

   GCC 2.96 and GNU Make. `alphaev6-unknown-linux-gnu`, `alphaev67-unknown-linux-gnu`.

5. SuSE Linux 7.2a

   GCC 3.0 and GNU Make. `ia64-unknown-linux-gnu`.

6. SuSE Linux

   GCC 3.2.2 and GNU Make. `x86_64-unknown-linux-gnu` (AMD64 Opteron "Melody").

7. SuSE Enterprise Server 9 on IBM OpenPower 720

   GCC 3.3.3 and GNU Make. `powerpc64-unknown-linux-gnu`.

8. RedHat Linux 7.2

   GCC 2.96 and GNU Make. `alphaev6-unknown-linux-gnu`, `alphaev67-unknown-linux-gnu`, `ia64-unknown-linux-gnu`.

9. RedHat Linux 8.0

   GCC 3.2 and GNU Make. `i686-pc-linux-gnu`.

10. RedHat Advanced Server 2.1

    GCC 2.96 and GNU Make. `i686-pc-linux-gnu`.

11. Slackware Linux 8.0.01

    GCC 2.95.3 and GNU Make. `i686-pc-linux-gnu`.

12. Mandrake Linux 9.0

    GCC 3.2 and GNU Make. `i686-pc-linux-gnu`.

13. IRIX 6.5

    MIPS C compiler, IRIX Make. `mips-sgi-irix6.5`.

14. AIX 4.3.2

    IBM C for AIX compiler, AIX Make. `rs6000-ibm-aix4.3.2.0`.

15. Microsoft Windows 2000 (Cygwin)

    GCC 3.2, GNU make. `i686-pc-cygwin`.

16. HP-UX 11

    HP-UX C compiler and HP Make. `ia64-hp-hpux11.22`, `hppa2.0w-hp-hpux11.11`.

17. SUN Solaris 2.7

    GCC 3.0.4 and GNU Make. `sparc-sun-solaris2.7`.

18. SUN Solaris 2.8

    Sun WorkShop Compiler C 6.0 and SUN Make. `sparc-sun-solaris2.8`.

19. SUN Solaris 2.9

    Sun Forte Developer 7 C compiler and GNU Make. `sparc-sun-solaris2.9`.

20. NetBSD 1.6

    GCC 2.95.3 and GNU Make. `alpha-unknown-netbsd1.6`, `i386-unknown-netbsdelf1.6`.

21. OpenBSD 3.1 and 3.2

    GCC 2.95.3 and GNU Make. `alpha-unknown-openbsd3.1`, `i386-unknown-openbsd3.1`.

22. FreeBSD 4.7 and 4.8

    GCC 2.95.4 and GNU Make. `alpha-unknown-freebsd4.7`, `alpha-unknown-freebsd4.8`, `i386-unknown-freebsd4.7`, `i386-unknown-freebsd4.8`.

23. MacOS X 10.2 Server Edition

    GCC 3.1 and GNU Make. `powerpc-apple-darwin6.5`.

24. MacOS X 10.4 "Tiger" with Xcode 2.0

    GCC 4.0 and GNU Make. `powerpc-apple-darwin8.0`.

25. Cross compiled to uClinux/uClibc on Motorola Coldfire

    GCC 3.4 and GNU Make `m68k-uclinux-elf`.

26. Cross compiled to ARM using Glibc

    GCC 2.95 and GNU Make `arm-linux`.

27. Cross compiled to Mingw32.

    GCC 3.4.4 and GNU Make `i586-mingw32msvc`.

28. OS/2

    GCC.

If you use Libidn on, or port Libidn to, a new platform please report it to the author.

1.5 Getting help

A mailing list where users of Libidn may help each other exists, and you can reach it by sending e-mail to `help-libidn@gnu.org`. Archives of the mailing list discussions, and an interface to manage subscriptions, is available through the World Wide Web at `http://lists.gnu.org/mailman/listinfo/help-libidn`.

1.6 Commercial Support

Commercial support is available for users of GNU Libidn. The kind of support that can be purchased may include:

- Implement new features. Such as country code specific profiling to support a restricted subset of Unicode.
- Port Libidn to new platforms. This could include porting Libidn to an embedded platforms that may need memory or size optimization.
- Integrating IDN support in your existing project.
- System design of components related to IDN.

If you are interested, please write to:

Simon Josefsson Datakonsult AB
Hagagatan 24
113 47 Stockholm
Sweden

E-mail: simon@josefsson.org

If your company provides support related to GNU Libidn and would like to be mentioned here, contact the author (see Section 1.8 [Bug Reports], page 7).

1.7 Downloading and Installing

The package can be downloaded from several places, including:

ftp://alpha.gnu.org/pub/gnu/libidn/

The latest version is stored in a file, e.g., 'libidn-1.32.tar.gz' where the '1.32' value is the highest version number in the directory.

The package is then extracted, configured and built like many other packages that use Autoconf. For detailed information on configuring and building it, refer to the INSTALL file that is part of the distribution archive.

Here is an example terminal session that download, configure, build and install the package. You will need a few basic tools, such as 'sh', 'make' and 'cc'.

```
$ wget -q ftp://alpha.gnu.org/pub/gnu/libidn/libidn-1.32.tar.gz
$ tar xfz libidn-1.32.tar.gz
$ cd libidn-1.32/
$ ./configure
...
$ make
...
$ make install
...
```

After that Libidn should be properly installed and ready for use.

A few configure options may be relevant, summarized in the table.

--enable-java

> Build the Java port into a *.JAR file. See Chapter 12 [Java API], page 58, for more information.

--disable-tld

> Disable the TLD module. This would typically only be useful if you are building on a memory restricted platforms. See Chapter 7 [TLD Functions], page 31, for more information.

--enable-csharp[=IMPL]

> Build the C# port into a *.DLL file. See Chapter 13 [C# API], page 61, for more information. Here, IMPL is pnet or mono, indicating whether the PNET cscc compiler or the Mono mcs compiler should be used, respectively.

--disable-valgrind-tests

> Disable running the self-checks under Valgrind (http://valgrind.org/). Normally Valgrind does not cause problems and can detect some severe memory

errors. If you are getting errors from Valgrind that are caused by the compiler or libc (possibly as a result of special optimization flags), you may use this option to disable the use of Valgrind.

For the complete list, refer to the output from `configure --help`.

1.7.1 Installing under Windows

There are two ways to build Libidn on Windows: via MinGW or via Visual Studio.

With MinGW, you can build a Libidn DLL and use it from other applications. After installing MinGW (`http://mingw.org/`) follow the generic installation instructions (see Section 1.7 [Downloading and Installing], page 6). The DLL is installed by default.

For information on how to use the DLL in other applications, see: `http://www.mingw.org/mingwfaq.shtml#faq-msvcdll`.

You can build Libidn as a native Visual Studio C++ project. This allows you to build the code for other platforms that VS supports, such as Windows Mobile. You need Visual Studio 2005 or later.

First download and unpack the archive as described in the generic installation instructions (see Section 1.7 [Downloading and Installing], page 6). Don't run `./configure`. Instead, start Visual Studio and open the project file `windows/libidn.sln` inside the Libidn directory. You should be able to build the project using Build Project.

Output libraries will be written into the `windows/lib` (or `windows/lib/debug` for Debug versions) folder.

When working with Windows you may want to look into the special memory handling functions that may be needed (see Section 2.6 [Memory handling under Windows], page 12).

1.8 Bug Reports

If you think you have found a bug in Libidn, please investigate it and report it.

- Please make sure that the bug is really in Libidn, and preferably also check that it hasn't already been fixed in the latest version.
- You have to send us a test case that makes it possible for us to reproduce the bug.
- You also have to explain what is wrong; if you get a crash, or if the results printed are not good and in that case, in what way. Make sure that the bug report includes all information you would need to fix this kind of bug for someone else.

Please make an effort to produce a self-contained report, with something definite that can be tested or debugged. Vague queries or piecemeal messages are difficult to act on and don't help the development effort.

If your bug report is good, we will do our best to help you to get a corrected version of the software; if the bug report is poor, we won't do anything about it (apart from asking you to send better bug reports).

If you think something in this manual is unclear, or downright incorrect, or if the language needs to be improved, please also send a note.

Send your bug report to:

'bug-libidn@gnu.org'

1.9 Contributing

If you want to submit a patch for inclusion – from solve a typo you discovered, up to adding support for a new feature – you should submit it as a bug report (see Section 1.8 [Bug Reports], page 7). There are some things that you can do to increase the chances for it to be included in the official package.

Unless your patch is very small (say, under 10 lines) we require that you assign the copyright of your work to the Free Software Foundation. This is to protect the freedom of the project. If you have not already signed papers, we will send you the necessary information when you submit your contribution.

For contributions that doesn't consist of actual programming code, the only guidelines are common sense. Use it.

For code contributions, a number of style guides will help you:

- Coding Style. Follow the GNU Standards document (see Section "top" in standards).

  If you normally code using another coding standard, there is no problem, but you should use 'indent' to reformat the code (see Section "top" in indent) before submitting your work.

- Use the unified diff format 'diff -u'.

- Return errors. No reason whatsoever should abort the execution of the library. Even memory allocation errors, e.g. when malloc return NULL, should work although result in an error code.

- Design with thread safety in mind. Don't use global variables and the like.

- Avoid using the C math library. It causes problems for embedded implementations, and in most situations it is very easy to avoid using it.

- Document your functions. Use comments before each function headers, that, if properly formatted, are extracted into GTK-DOC web pages. Don't forget to update the Texinfo manual as well.

- Supply a ChangeLog and NEWS entries, where appropriate.

2 Preparation

To use 'Libidn', you have to perform some changes to your sources and the build system. The necessary changes are small and explained in the following sections. At the end of this chapter, it is described how the library is initialized, and how the requirements of the library are verified.

A faster way to find out how to adapt your application for use with 'Libidn' may be to look at the examples at the end of this manual (see Chapter 9 [Examples], page 38).

2.1 Header

The library contains a few independent parts, and each part export the interfaces (data types and functions) in a header file. You must include the appropriate header files in all programs using the library, either directly or through some other header file, like this:

        #include <stringprep.h>

The header files and the functions they define are categorized as follows:

stringprep.h

> The low-level stringprep API entry point. For IDN applications, this is usually invoked via IDNA. Some applications, specifically non-IDN ones, may want to prepare strings directly though, and should include this header file.
>
> The name space of the stringprep part of Libidn is `stringprep*` for function names, `Stringprep*` for data types and `STRINGPREP_*` for other symbols. In addition, `_stringprep*` is reserved for internal use and should never be used by applications.

punycode.h

> The entry point to Punycode encoding and decoding functions. Normally punycode is used via the idna.h interface, but some application may want to perform raw punycode operations.
>
> The name space of the punycode part of Libidn is `punycode_*` for function names, `Punycode*` for data types and `PUNYCODE_*` for other symbols. In addition, `_punycode*` is reserved for internal use and should never be used by applications.

idna.h

> The entry point to the IDNA functions. This is the normal entry point for applications that need IDN functionality.
>
> The name space of the IDNA part of Libidn is `idna_*` for function names, `Idna*` for data types and `IDNA_*` for other symbols. In addition, `_idna*` is reserved for internal use and should never be used by applications.

tld.h

> The entry point to the TLD functions. Normal applications are not expected to need this functionality, but it is present for applications that are used by TLDs to validate customer input.
>
> The name space of the TLD part of Libidn is `tld_*` for function names, `Tld_*` for data types and `TLD_*` for other symbols. In addition, `_tld*` is reserved for internal use and should never be used by applications.

pr29.h

> The entry point to the PR29 functions. These functions are used to detect "problem sequences" (see Chapter 8 [PR29 Functions], page 36), mostly for use in security critical applications.
>
> The name space of the PR29 part of Libidn is `pr29_*` for function names, `Pr29_*` for data types and `PR29_*` for other symbols. In addition, `_pr29*` is reserved for internal use and should never be used by applications.

idn-free.h

> The entry point to the Windows memory de-allocation function (see Section 2.6 [Memory handling under Windows], page 12). It contains only one function `idn_free`.

All header files defined and use the symbol `IDNAPI` to decorate the API functions.

2.2 Initialization

Libidn is stateless and does not need any initialization.

2.3 Version Check

It is often desirable to check that the version of 'Libidn' used is indeed one which fits all requirements. Even with binary compatibility new features may have been introduced but due to problem with the dynamic linker an old version is actually used. So you may want to check that the version is okay right after program startup.

stringprep_check_version

const char * stringprep_check_version (*const char *__   [Function]
        req_version)

> *req_version*: Required version number, or NULL.
>
> Check that the version of the library is at minimum the requested one and return the version string; return NULL if the condition is not satisfied. If a NULL is passed to this function, no check is done, but the version string is simply returned.
>
> See `STRINGPREP_VERSION` for a suitable `req_version` string.
>
> Return value: Version string of run-time library, or NULL if the run-time library does not meet the required version number.

The normal way to use the function is to put something similar to the following first in your `main`:

```
if (!stringprep_check_version (STRINGPREP_VERSION))
  {
    printf ("stringprep_check_version() failed:\n"
            "Header file incompatible with shared library.\n");
    exit(EXIT_FAILURE);
  }
```

2.4 Building the source

If you want to compile a source file including e.g. the 'idna.h' header file, you must make sure that the compiler can find it in the directory hierarchy. This is accomplished by adding the path to the directory in which the header file is located to the compilers include file search path (via the -I option).

However, the path to the include file is determined at the time the source is configured. To solve this problem, 'Libidn' uses the external package **pkg-config** that knows the path to the include file and other configuration options. The options that need to be added to the compiler invocation at compile time are output by the --cflags option to **pkg-config libidn**. The following example shows how it can be used at the command line:

```
gcc -c foo.c `pkg-config libidn --cflags`
```

Adding the output of 'pkg-config libidn --cflags' to the compilers command line will ensure that the compiler can find e.g. the idna.h header file.

A similar problem occurs when linking the program with the library. Again, the compiler has to find the library files. For this to work, the path to the library files has to be added to the library search path (via the -L option). For this, the option --libs to **pkg-config libidn** can be used. For convenience, this option also outputs all other options that are required to link the program with the 'libidn' library. The example shows how to link foo.o with the 'libidn' library to a program foo.

```
gcc -o foo foo.o `pkg-config libidn --libs`
```

Of course you can also combine both examples to a single command by specifying both options to pkg-config:

```
gcc -o foo foo.c `pkg-config libidn --cflags --libs`
```

2.5 Autoconf tests

If your project uses Autoconf (see Section "top" in autoconf) to check for installed libraries, you might find the following snippet illustrative. It add a new **configure** parameter --with-libidn, and check for idna.h and '-lidn' (possibly below the directory specified as the optional argument to --with-libidn), and define the CPP symbol LIBIDN if the library is found. The default behaviour is to search for the library and enable the functionality (that is, define the symbol) when the library is found, but if you wish to make the default behaviour of your package be that Libidn is not used (even if it is installed on the system), change 'libidn=yes' to 'libidn=no' on the third line.

```
AC_ARG_WITH(libidn, AC_HELP_STRING([--with-libidn=[DIR]],
                                 [Support IDN (needs GNU Libidn)]),
    libidn=$withval, libidn=yes)
if test "$libidn" != "no"; then
  if test "$libidn" != "yes"; then
    LDFLAGS="${LDFLAGS} -L$libidn/lib"
    CPPFLAGS="${CPPFLAGS} -I$libidn/include"
  fi
  AC_CHECK_HEADER(idna.h,
    AC_CHECK_LIB(idn, stringprep_check_version,
      [libidn=yes LIBS="${LIBS} -lidn"], libidn=no),
```

```
      libidn=no)
fi
if test "$libidn" != "no" ; then
  AC_DEFINE(LIBIDN, 1, [Define to 1 if you want IDN support.])
else
  AC_MSG_WARN([Libidn not found])
fi
AC_MSG_CHECKING([if Libidn should be used])
AC_MSG_RESULT($libidn)
```

If you require that your users have installed **pkg-config** (which I cannot recommend generally), the above can be done more easily as follows.

```
AC_ARG_WITH(libidn, AC_HELP_STRING([--with-libidn=[DIR]],
                               [Support IDN (needs GNU Libidn)]),
  libidn=$withval, libidn=yes)
if test "$libidn" != "no" ; then
  PKG_CHECK_MODULES(LIBIDN, libidn >= 0.0.0, [libidn=yes], [libidn=no])
  if test "$libidn" != "yes" ; then
    libidn=no
    AC_MSG_WARN([Libidn not found])
  else
    libidn=yes
    AC_DEFINE(LIBIDN, 1, [Define to 1 if you want Libidn.])
  fi
fi
AC_MSG_CHECKING([if Libidn should be used])
AC_MSG_RESULT($libidn)
```

2.6 Memory handling under Windows

Several functions in the library allocates memory. The memory is expected to be de-allocated using the **free** function. Under Windows, it is sometimes necessary to de-allocate memory in the same module that allocated a memory region. The reason is that different modules use separate heap memory regions. To solve this problem we provide a function to de-allocate memory inside the library.

Note that we do not recommend using this interface generally if you do not care about Windows portability.

2.7 Header file idn-free.h

To use the function explained in this chapter, you need to include the file **idn-free.h** using:

```
#include <idn-free.h>
```

2.8 Memory de-allocation function

idn_free

`void` `idn_free` (*void* `* ptr`)   [Function]

> *ptr*: memory region to deallocate, or `NULL` .
>
> Deallocates memory region by calling `free()` . If `ptr` is `NULL` no operation is performed.
>
> Normally applications de-allocate strings allocated by libidn by calling `free()` directly. Under Windows, different parts of the same application may use different heap memory, and then it is important to deallocate memory allocated within the same module that allocated it. This function makes that possible.

3 Utility Functions

The rest of this library makes extensive use of Unicode characters. In order to interface this library with the outside world, your application may need to make various Unicode transformations.

3.1 Header file `stringprep.h`

To use the functions explained in this chapter, you need to include the file **stringprep.h** using:

```
#include <stringprep.h>
```

3.2 Unicode Encoding Transformation

stringprep_unichar_to_utf8

int **stringprep_unichar_to_utf8** (*uint32_t c*, *char * outbuf*)   [Function]
    c: a ISO10646 character code

outbuf: output buffer, must have at least 6 bytes of space. If NULL , the length will be computed and returned and nothing will be written to **outbuf** .

Converts a single character to UTF-8.

Return value: number of bytes written.

stringprep_utf8_to_unichar

uint32_t **stringprep_utf8_to_unichar** (*const char * p*)   [Function]
    p: a pointer to Unicode character encoded as UTF-8

Converts a sequence of bytes encoded as UTF-8 to a Unicode character. If **p** does not point to a valid UTF-8 encoded character, results are undefined.

Return value: the resulting character.

stringprep_ucs4_to_utf8

char * **stringprep_ucs4_to_utf8** (*const uint32_t * str*, *ssize_t len*,   [Function]
        size_t * items_read, *size_t * items_written*)
    str: a UCS-4 encoded string

len: the maximum length of **str** to use. If **len** < 0, then the string is terminated with a 0 character.

items_read: location to store number of characters read read, or NULL .

items_written: location to store number of bytes written or NULL . The value here stored does not include the trailing 0 byte.

Convert a string from a 32-bit fixed width representation as UCS-4. to UTF-8. The result will be terminated with a 0 byte.

Return value: a pointer to a newly allocated UTF-8 string. This value must be deallocated by the caller. If an error occurs, NULL will be returned.

stringprep_utf8_to_ucs4

uint32_t * stringprep_utf8_to_ucs4 (*const char* * *str*, *ssize_t* **len**,   [Function]
      size_t * *items_written*)

> *str*: a UTF-8 encoded string
>
> *len*: the maximum length of **str** to use. If **len** < 0, then the string is nul-terminated.
>
> *items_written*: location to store the number of characters in the result, or **NULL** .
>
> Convert a string from UTF-8 to a 32-bit fixed width representation as UCS-4. The function now performs error checking to verify that the input is valid UTF-8 (before it was documented to not do error checking).
>
> Return value: a pointer to a newly allocated UCS-4 string. This value must be deallocated by the caller.

3.3 Unicode Normalization

stringprep_ucs4_nfkc_normalize

uint32_t * stringprep_ucs4_nfkc_normalize (*const uint32_t* *   [Function]
      str, *ssize_t* **len**)

> *str*: a Unicode string.
>
> *len*: length of **str** array, or -1 if **str** is nul-terminated.
>
> Converts a UCS4 string into canonical form, see **stringprep_utf8_nfkc_normalize()** for more information.
>
> Return value: a newly allocated Unicode string, that is the NFKC normalized form of **str** .

stringprep_utf8_nfkc_normalize

char * stringprep_utf8_nfkc_normalize (*const char* * *str*, *ssize_t*   [Function]
      len)

> *str*: a UTF-8 encoded string.
>
> *len*: length of **str** , in bytes, or -1 if **str** is nul-terminated.
>
> Converts a string into canonical form, standardizing such issues as whether a character with an accent is represented as a base character and combining accent or as a single precomposed character.
>
> The normalization mode is NFKC (ALL COMPOSE). It standardizes differences that do not affect the text content, such as the above-mentioned accent representation. It standardizes the "compatibility" characters in Unicode, such as SUPERSCRIPT THREE to the standard forms (in this case DIGIT THREE). Formatting information may be lost but for most text operations such characters should be considered the same. It returns a result with composed forms rather than a maximally decomposed form.
>
> Return value: a newly allocated string, that is the NFKC normalized form of **str** .

3.4 Character Set Conversion

stringprep_locale_charset

const char * stringprep_locale_charset (*void*)   [Function]
    Find out current locale charset. The function respect the CHARSET environment variable, but typically uses nl_langinfo(CODESET) when it is supported. It fall back on "ASCII" if CHARSET isn't set and nl_langinfo isn't supported or return anything.

    Note that this function return the application's locale's preferred charset (or thread's locale's preffered charset, if your system support thread-specific locales). It does not return what the system may be using. Thus, if you receive data from external sources you cannot in general use this function to guess what charset it is encoded in. Use stringprep_convert from the external representation into the charset returned by this function, to have data in the locale encoding.

    Return value: Return the character set used by the current locale. It will never return NULL, but use "ASCII" as a fallback.

stringprep_convert

char * stringprep_convert (*const char * str*, *const char **   [Function]
    to_codeset, *const char * from_codeset*)
    str: input zero-terminated string.

    to_codeset: name of destination character set.

    from_codeset: name of origin character set, as used by str .

    Convert the string from one character set to another using the system's iconv() function.

    Return value: Returns newly allocated zero-terminated string which is str transcoded into to_codeset.

stringprep_locale_to_utf8

char * stringprep_locale_to_utf8 (*const char * str*)   [Function]
    str: input zero terminated string.

    Convert string encoded in the locale's character set into UTF-8 by using stringprep_convert() .

    Return value: Returns newly allocated zero-terminated string which is str transcoded into UTF-8.

stringprep_utf8_to_locale

char * stringprep_utf8_to_locale (*const char * str*)   [Function]
    str: input zero terminated string.

    Convert string encoded in UTF-8 into the locale's character set by using stringprep_convert() .

    Return value: Returns newly allocated zero-terminated string which is str transcoded into the locale's character set.

4 Stringprep Functions

Stringprep describes a framework for preparing Unicode text strings in order to increase the likelihood that string input and string comparison work in ways that make sense for typical users throughout the world. The stringprep protocol is useful for protocol identifier values, company and personal names, internationalized domain names, and other text strings.

4.1 Header file `stringprep.h`

To use the functions explained in this chapter, you need to include the file `stringprep.h` using:

```
#include <stringprep.h>
```

4.2 Defining A Stringprep Profile

Further types and structures are defined for applications that want to specify their own stringprep profile. As these are fairly obscure, and by necessity tied to the implementation, we do not document them here. Look into the `stringprep.h` header file, and the `profiles.c` source code for the details.

4.3 Control Flags

`Stringprep_profile_flags STRINGPREP_NO_NFKC`   [Stringprep flags]
> Disable the NFKC normalization, as well as selecting the non-NFKC case folding tables. Usually the profile specifies BIDI and NFKC settings, and applications should not override it unless in special situations.

`Stringprep_profile_flags STRINGPREP_NO_BIDI`   [Stringprep flags]
> Disable the BIDI step. Usually the profile specifies BIDI and NFKC settings, and applications should not override it unless in special situations.

`Stringprep_profile_flags STRINGPREP_NO_UNASSIGNED`   [Stringprep flags]
> Make the library return with an error if string contains unassigned characters according to profile.

4.4 Core Functions

stringprep_4i

int `stringprep_4i` (*uint32_t* * `ucs4`, *size_t* * `len`, *size_t* `maxucs4len`,   [Function]
> *Stringprep_profile_flags* `flags`, const *Stringprep_profile* * `profile`)
> *ucs4*: input/output array with string to prepare.
>
> *len*: on input, length of input array with Unicode code points, on exit, length of output array with Unicode code points.
>
> *maxucs4len*: maximum length of input/output array.
>
> *flags*: a `Stringprep_profile_flags` value, or 0.
>
> *profile*: pointer to `Stringprep_profile` to use.

Prepare the input UCS-4 string according to the stringprep profile, and write back the result to the input string.

The input is not required to be zero terminated (ucs4 [len] = 0). The output will not be zero terminated unless ucs4 [len] = 0. Instead, see `stringprep_4zi()` if your input is zero terminated or if you want the output to be.

Since the stringprep operation can expand the string, `maxucs4len` indicate how large the buffer holding the string is. This function will not read or write to code points outside that size.

The `flags` are one of `Stringprep_profile_flags` values, or 0.

The `profile` contain the `Stringprep_profile` instructions to perform. Your application can define new profiles, possibly re-using the generic stringprep tables that always will be part of the library, or use one of the currently supported profiles.

Return value: Returns `STRINGPREP_OK` iff successful, or an `Stringprep_rc` error code.

stringprep_4zi

int stringprep_4zi (*uint32_t* * *ucs4*, *size_t* maxucs4len,   [Function]
        Stringprep_profile_flags **flags**, *const Stringprep_profile* * **profile**)

ucs4: input/output array with zero terminated string to prepare.

maxucs4len: maximum length of input/output array.

flags: a `Stringprep_profile_flags` value, or 0.

profile: pointer to `Stringprep_profile` to use.

Prepare the input zero terminated UCS-4 string according to the stringprep profile, and write back the result to the input string.

Since the stringprep operation can expand the string, `maxucs4len` indicate how large the buffer holding the string is. This function will not read or write to code points outside that size.

The `flags` are one of `Stringprep_profile_flags` values, or 0.

The `profile` contain the `Stringprep_profile` instructions to perform. Your application can define new profiles, possibly re-using the generic stringprep tables that always will be part of the library, or use one of the currently supported profiles.

Return value: Returns `STRINGPREP_OK` iff successful, or an `Stringprep_rc` error code.

stringprep

int stringprep (*char* * *in*, *size_t* maxlen, *Stringprep_profile_flags*   [Function]
        flags, *const Stringprep_profile* * **profile**)

in: input/ouput array with string to prepare.

maxlen: maximum length of input/output array.

flags: a `Stringprep_profile_flags` value, or 0.

profile: pointer to `Stringprep_profile` to use.

Prepare the input zero terminated UTF-8 string according to the stringprep profile, and write back the result to the input string.

Note that you must convert strings entered in the systems locale into UTF-8 before using this function, see `stringprep_locale_to_utf8()` .

Since the stringprep operation can expand the string, `maxlen` indicate how large the buffer holding the string is. This function will not read or write to characters outside that size.

The `flags` are one of `Stringprep_profile_flags` values, or 0.

The `profile` contain the `Stringprep_profile` instructions to perform. Your application can define new profiles, possibly re-using the generic stringprep tables that always will be part of the library, or use one of the currently supported profiles.

Return value: Returns `STRINGPREP_OK` iff successful, or an error code.

stringprep_profile

`int stringprep_profile` (*const char * in, char ** out, const char **   [Function]
    profile, Stringprep_profile_flags flags)
in: input array with UTF-8 string to prepare.

out: output variable with pointer to newly allocate string.

profile: name of stringprep profile to use.

flags: a `Stringprep_profile_flags` value, or 0.

Prepare the input zero terminated UTF-8 string according to the stringprep profile, and return the result in a newly allocated variable.

Note that you must convert strings entered in the systems locale into UTF-8 before using this function, see `stringprep_locale_to_utf8()` .

The output `out` variable must be deallocated by the caller.

The `flags` are one of `Stringprep_profile_flags` values, or 0.

The `profile` specifies the name of the stringprep profile to use. It must be one of the internally supported stringprep profiles.

Return value: Returns `STRINGPREP_OK` iff successful, or an error code.

4.5 Error Handling

stringprep_strerror

`const char * stringprep_strerror` (*Stringprep_rc rc*)   [Function]
    rc: a `Stringprep_rc` return code.

Convert a return code integer to a text string. This string can be used to output a diagnostic message to the user.

STRINGPREP_OK: Successful operation. This value is guaranteed to always be zero, the remaining ones are only guaranteed to hold non-zero values, for logical comparison purposes.

STRINGPREP_CONTAINS_UNASSIGNED: String contain unassigned Unicode code points, which is forbidden by the profile.

STRINGPREP_CONTAINS_PROHIBITED: String contain code points prohibited by the profile.

STRINGPREP_BIDI_BOTH_L_AND_RAL: String contain code points with conflicting bidirection category.

STRINGPREP_BIDI_LEADTRAIL_NOT_RAL: Leading and trailing character in string not of proper bidirectional category.

STRINGPREP_BIDI_CONTAINS_PROHIBITED: Contains prohibited code points detected by bidirectional code.

STRINGPREP_TOO_SMALL_BUFFER: Buffer handed to function was too small. This usually indicate a problem in the calling application.

STRINGPREP_PROFILE_ERROR: The stringprep profile was inconsistent. This usually indicate an internal error in the library.

STRINGPREP_FLAG_ERROR: The supplied flag conflicted with profile. This usually indicate a problem in the calling application.

STRINGPREP_UNKNOWN_PROFILE: The supplied profile name was not known to the library.

STRINGPREP_ICONV_ERROR: Could not convert string in locale encoding.

STRINGPREP_NFKC_FAILED: The Unicode NFKC operation failed. This usually indicate an internal error in the library.

STRINGPREP_MALLOC_ERROR: The `malloc()` was out of memory. This is usually a fatal error.

Return value: Returns a pointer to a statically allocated string containing a description of the error with the return code `rc` .

4.6 Stringprep Profile Macros

int stringprep_nameprep_no_unassigned (*char * in*, *int maxlen*)   [Function]
> *in*: input/ouput array with string to prepare.
>
> *maxlen*: maximum length of input/output array.
>
> Prepare the input UTF-8 string according to the nameprep profile. The AllowUnassigned flag is false, use `stringprep_nameprep` for true AllowUnassigned. Returns 0 iff successful, or an error code.

int stringprep_iscsi (*char * in*, *int maxlen*)   [Function]
> *in*: input/ouput array with string to prepare.
>
> *maxlen*: maximum length of input/output array.
>
> Prepare the input UTF-8 string according to the draft iSCSI stringprep profile. Returns 0 iff successful, or an error code.

int stringprep_plain (*char * in*, *int maxlen*)   [Function]
> *in*: input/ouput array with string to prepare.
>
> *maxlen*: maximum length of input/output array.
>
> Prepare the input UTF-8 string according to the draft SASL ANONYMOUS profile. Returns 0 iff successful, or an error code.

int stringprep_xmpp_nodeprep (*char * in*, *int maxlen*)   [Function]

   in: input/ouput array with string to prepare.

   maxlen: maximum length of input/output array.

   Prepare the input UTF-8 string according to the draft XMPP node identifier profile. Returns 0 iff successful, or an error code.

int stringprep_xmpp_resourceprep (*char * in*, *int maxlen*)   [Function]

   in: input/ouput array with string to prepare.

   maxlen: maximum length of input/output array.

   Prepare the input UTF-8 string according to the draft XMPP resource identifier profile. Returns 0 iff successful, or an error code.

5 Punycode Functions

Punycode is a simple and efficient transfer encoding syntax designed for use with Internationalized Domain Names in Applications. It uniquely and reversibly transforms a Unicode string into an ASCII string. ASCII characters in the Unicode string are represented literally, and non-ASCII characters are represented by ASCII characters that are allowed in host name labels (letters, digits, and hyphens). A general algorithm called Bootstring allows a string of basic code points to uniquely represent any string of code points drawn from a larger set. Punycode is an instance of Bootstring that uses particular parameter values, appropriate for IDNA.

5.1 Header file punycode.h

To use the functions explained in this chapter, you need to include the file punycode.h using:

```
#include <punycode.h>
```

5.2 Unicode Code Point Data Type

The punycode function uses a special type to denote Unicode code points. It is guaranteed to always be a 32 bit unsigned integer.

uint32_t punycode_uint   [Punycode Unicode code point]
    A unsigned integer that hold Unicode code points.

5.3 Core Functions

Note that the current implementation will fail if the input_length exceed 4294967295 (the size of punycode_uint). This restriction may be removed in the future. Meanwhile applications are encouraged to not depend on this problem, and use sizeof to initialize input_length and output_length.

    The functions provided are the following two entry points:

punycode_encode

int punycode_encode (*size_t* input_length, *const punycode_uint* []   [Function]
      input, *const unsigned char* [] case_flags, *size_t* * output_length, *char* []
      output)
    input_length: The number of code points in the input array and the number of flags in the case_flags array.

    input: An array of code points. They are presumed to be Unicode code points, but that is not strictly REQUIRED. The array contains code points, not code units. UTF-16 uses code units D800 through DFFF to refer to code points 10000..10FFFF. The code points D800..DFFF do not occur in any valid Unicode string. The code points that can occur in Unicode strings (0..D7FF and E000..10FFFF) are also called Unicode scalar values.

    case_flags: A NULL pointer or an array of boolean values parallel to the input array. Nonzero (true, flagged) suggests that the corresponding Unicode character be forced to uppercase after being decoded (if possible), and zero (false, unflagged) suggests that it be forced to lowercase (if possible). ASCII code points (0..7F) are encoded literally, except that ASCII letters are forced to uppercase or lowercase according to the corresponding case flags. If `case_flags` is a `NULL` pointer then ASCII letters are left as they are, and other code points are treated as unflagged.

output_length: The caller passes in the maximum number of ASCII code points that it can receive. On successful return it will contain the number of ASCII code points actually output.

output: An array of ASCII code points. It is *not* null-terminated; it will contain zeros if and only if the `input` contains zeros. (Of course the caller can leave room for a terminator and add one if needed.)

Converts a sequence of code points (presumed to be Unicode code points) to Punycode.

Return value: The return value can be any of the `Punycode_status` values defined above except `PUNYCODE_BAD_INPUT` . If not `PUNYCODE_SUCCESS` , then `output_size` and `output` might contain garbage.

punycode_decode

`int punycode_decode` (*size_t* `input_length`, *const char* [] `input`, *size_t*   [Function]
         * `output_length`, *punycode_uint* [] `output`, *unsigned char* [] `case_flags`)
input_length: The number of ASCII code points in the `input` array.

input: An array of ASCII code points (0..7F).

output_length: The caller passes in the maximum number of code points that it can receive into the `output` array (which is also the maximum number of flags that it can receive into the `case_flags` array, if `case_flags` is not a `NULL` pointer). On successful return it will contain the number of code points actually output (which is also the number of flags actually output, if case_flags is not a null pointer). The decoder will never need to output more code points than the number of ASCII code points in the input, because of the way the encoding is defined. The number of code points output cannot exceed the maximum possible value of a punycode_uint, even if the supplied `output_length` is greater than that.

output: An array of code points like the input argument of `punycode_encode()` (see above).

case_flags: A `NULL` pointer (if the flags are not needed by the caller) or an array of boolean values parallel to the `output` array. Nonzero (true, flagged) suggests that the corresponding Unicode character be forced to uppercase by the caller (if possible), and zero (false, unflagged) suggests that it be forced to lowercase (if possible). ASCII code points (0..7F) are output already in the proper case, but their flags will be set appropriately so that applying the flags would be harmless.

Converts Punycode to a sequence of code points (presumed to be Unicode code points).

Return value: The return value can be any of the `Punycode_status` values defined above. If not `PUNYCODE_SUCCESS` , then `output_length` , `output` , and `case_flags` might contain garbage.

5.4 Error Handling

punycode_strerror

const char * punycode_strerror (*Punycode_status* **rc**) [Function]

> *rc*: an Punycode_status return code.

> Convert a return code integer to a text string. This string can be used to output a diagnostic message to the user.

> **PUNYCODE_SUCCESS:** Successful operation. This value is guaranteed to always be zero, the remaining ones are only guaranteed to hold non-zero values, for logical comparison purposes.

> **PUNYCODE_BAD_INPUT:** Input is invalid.

> **PUNYCODE_BIG_OUTPUT:** Output would exceed the space provided.

> **PUNYCODE_OVERFLOW:** Input needs wider integers to process.

> Return value: Returns a pointer to a statically allocated string containing a description of the error with the return code **rc** .

6 IDNA Functions

Until now, there has been no standard method for domain names to use characters outside the ASCII repertoire. The IDNA document defines internationalized domain names (IDNs) and a mechanism called IDNA for handling them in a standard fashion. IDNs use characters drawn from a large repertoire (Unicode), but IDNA allows the non-ASCII characters to be represented using only the ASCII characters already allowed in so-called host names today. This backward-compatible representation is required in existing protocols like DNS, so that IDNs can be introduced with no changes to the existing infrastructure. IDNA is only meant for processing domain names, not free text.

6.1 Header file `idna.h`

To use the functions explained in this chapter, you need to include the file **idna.h** using:

```
#include <idna.h>
```

6.2 Control Flags

The IDNA `flags` parameter can take on the following values, or a bit-wise inclusive or of any subset of the parameters:

`Idna_flags IDNA_ALLOW_UNASSIGNED`   [Return code]
    Allow unassigned Unicode code points.

`Idna_flags IDNA_USE_STD3_ASCII_RULES`   [Return code]
    Check output to make sure it is a STD3 conforming host name.

6.3 Prefix String

`#define IDNA_ACE_PREFIX`   [Macro]
    String with the official IDNA prefix, xn--.

6.4 Core Functions

The idea behind the IDNA function names are as follows: the `idna_to_ascii_4i` and `idna_to_unicode_44i` functions are the core IDNA primitives. The 4 indicate that the function takes UCS-4 strings (i.e., Unicode code points encoded in a 32-bit unsigned integer type) of the specified length. The i indicate that the data is written "inline" into the buffer. This means the caller is responsible for allocating (and de-allocating) the string, and providing the library with the allocated length of the string. The output length is written in the output length variable. The remaining functions all contain the z indicator, which means the strings are zero terminated. All output strings are allocated by the library, and must be de-allocated by the caller. The 4 indicator again means that the string is UCS-4, the 8 means the strings are UTF-8 and the 1 indicator means the strings are encoded in the encoding used by the current locale.

The functions provided are the following entry points:

idna_to_ascii_4i

int **idna_to_ascii_4i** (*const uint32_t * in*, *size_t* **inlen**, *char * out*,   [Function]
     int **flags**)

in: input array with unicode code points.

inlen: length of input array with unicode code points.

out: output zero terminated string that must have room for at least 63 characters plus the terminating zero.

flags: an **Idna_flags** value, e.g., **IDNA_ALLOW_UNASSIGNED** or **IDNA_USE_STD3_ASCII_RULES** .

The ToASCII operation takes a sequence of Unicode code points that make up one domain label and transforms it into a sequence of code points in the ASCII range (0..7F). If ToASCII succeeds, the original sequence and the resulting sequence are equivalent labels.

It is important to note that the ToASCII operation can fail. ToASCII fails if any step of it fails. If any step of the ToASCII operation fails on any label in a domain name, that domain name MUST NOT be used as an internationalized domain name. The method for deadling with this failure is application-specific.

The inputs to ToASCII are a sequence of code points, the AllowUnassigned flag, and the UseSTD3ASCIIRules flag. The output of ToASCII is either a sequence of ASCII code points or a failure condition.

ToASCII never alters a sequence of code points that are all in the ASCII range to begin with (although it could fail). Applying the ToASCII operation multiple times has exactly the same effect as applying it just once.

Return value: Returns 0 on success, or an **Idna_rc** error code.

idna_to_unicode_44i

int **idna_to_unicode_44i** (*const uint32_t * in*, *size_t* **inlen**, *uint32_t*   [Function]
     * out, *size_t * outlen*, *int* **flags**)

in: input array with unicode code points.

inlen: length of input array with unicode code points.

out: output array with unicode code points.

outlen: on input, maximum size of output array with unicode code points, on exit, actual size of output array with unicode code points.

flags: an **Idna_flags** value, e.g., **IDNA_ALLOW_UNASSIGNED** or **IDNA_USE_STD3_ASCII_RULES** .

The ToUnicode operation takes a sequence of Unicode code points that make up one domain label and returns a sequence of Unicode code points. If the input sequence is a label in ACE form, then the result is an equivalent internationalized label that is not in ACE form, otherwise the original sequence is returned unaltered.

ToUnicode never fails. If any step fails, then the original input sequence is returned immediately in that step.

The Punycode decoder can never output more code points than it inputs, but Nameprep can, and therefore ToUnicode can. Note that the number of octets needed to represent a sequence of code points depends on the particular character encoding used.

The inputs to ToUnicode are a sequence of code points, the AllowUnassigned flag, and the UseSTD3ASCIIRules flag. The output of ToUnicode is always a sequence of Unicode code points.

Return value: Returns `Idna_rc` error condition, but it must only be used for debugging purposes. The output buffer is always guaranteed to contain the correct data according to the specification (sans malloc induced errors). NB! This means that you normally ignore the return code from this function, as checking it means breaking the standard.

6.5 Simplified ToASCII Interface

idna_to_ascii_4z

int **idna_to_ascii_4z** (*const uint32_t * input, char ** output, int*   [Function]
    flags)

input: zero terminated input Unicode string.

output: pointer to newly allocated output string.

flags: an `Idna_flags` value, e.g., `IDNA_ALLOW_UNASSIGNED` or `IDNA_USE_STD3_ASCII_RULES` .

Convert UCS-4 domain name to ASCII string. The domain name may contain several labels, separated by dots. The output buffer must be deallocated by the caller.

Return value: Returns `IDNA_SUCCESS` on success, or error code.

idna_to_ascii_8z

int **idna_to_ascii_8z** (*const char * input, char ** output, int*   [Function]
    flags)

input: zero terminated input UTF-8 string.

output: pointer to newly allocated output string.

flags: an `Idna_flags` value, e.g., `IDNA_ALLOW_UNASSIGNED` or `IDNA_USE_STD3_ASCII_RULES` .

Convert UTF-8 domain name to ASCII string. The domain name may contain several labels, separated by dots. The output buffer must be deallocated by the caller.

Return value: Returns `IDNA_SUCCESS` on success, or error code.

idna_to_ascii_lz

int **idna_to_ascii_lz** (*const char * input, char ** output, int*   [Function]
    flags)

input: zero terminated input string encoded in the current locale's character set.

output: pointer to newly allocated output string.

flags: an `Idna_flags` value, e.g., `IDNA_ALLOW_UNASSIGNED` or `IDNA_USE_STD3_ASCII_RULES` .

Convert domain name in the locale's encoding to ASCII string. The domain name may contain several labels, separated by dots. The output buffer must be deallocated by the caller.

Return value: Returns `IDNA_SUCCESS` on success, or error code.

6.6 Simplified ToUnicode Interface

idna_to_unicode_4z4z

int idna_to_unicode_4z4z (*const uint32_t * input*, *uint32_t **   [Function] output*, *int flags*)

input: zero-terminated Unicode string.

output: pointer to newly allocated output Unicode string.

flags: an `Idna_flags` value, e.g., `IDNA_ALLOW_UNASSIGNED` or `IDNA_USE_STD3_ ASCII_RULES` .

Convert possibly ACE encoded domain name in UCS-4 format into a UCS-4 string. The domain name may contain several labels, separated by dots. The output buffer must be deallocated by the caller.

Return value: Returns `IDNA_SUCCESS` on success, or error code.

idna_to_unicode_8z4z

int idna_to_unicode_8z4z (*const char * input*, *uint32_t ** output*,   [Function] *int flags*)

input: zero-terminated UTF-8 string.

output: pointer to newly allocated output Unicode string.

flags: an `Idna_flags` value, e.g., `IDNA_ALLOW_UNASSIGNED` or `IDNA_USE_STD3_ ASCII_RULES` .

Convert possibly ACE encoded domain name in UTF-8 format into a UCS-4 string. The domain name may contain several labels, separated by dots. The output buffer must be deallocated by the caller.

Return value: Returns `IDNA_SUCCESS` on success, or error code.

idna_to_unicode_8z8z

int idna_to_unicode_8z8z (*const char * input*, *char ** output*, *int*   [Function] *flags*)

input: zero-terminated UTF-8 string.

output: pointer to newly allocated output UTF-8 string.

flags: an `Idna_flags` value, e.g., `IDNA_ALLOW_UNASSIGNED` or `IDNA_USE_STD3_ ASCII_RULES` .

Convert possibly ACE encoded domain name in UTF-8 format into a UTF-8 string. The domain name may contain several labels, separated by dots. The output buffer must be deallocated by the caller.

Return value: Returns `IDNA_SUCCESS` on success, or error code.

idna_to_unicode_8zlz

int idna_to_unicode_8zlz (*const char * input, char ** output, int*   [Function]
    flags)

input: zero-terminated UTF-8 string.

output: pointer to newly allocated output string encoded in the current locale's character set.

flags: an `Idna_flags` value, e.g., `IDNA_ALLOW_UNASSIGNED` or `IDNA_USE_STD3_ASCII_RULES` .

Convert possibly ACE encoded domain name in UTF-8 format into a string encoded in the current locale's character set. The domain name may contain several labels, separated by dots. The output buffer must be deallocated by the caller.

Return value: Returns `IDNA_SUCCESS` on success, or error code.

idna_to_unicode_lzlz

int idna_to_unicode_lzlz (*const char * input, char ** output, int*   [Function]
    flags)

input: zero-terminated string encoded in the current locale's character set.

output: pointer to newly allocated output string encoded in the current locale's character set.

flags: an `Idna_flags` value, e.g., `IDNA_ALLOW_UNASSIGNED` or `IDNA_USE_STD3_ASCII_RULES` .

Convert possibly ACE encoded domain name in the locale's character set into a string encoded in the current locale's character set. The domain name may contain several labels, separated by dots. The output buffer must be deallocated by the caller.

Return value: Returns `IDNA_SUCCESS` on success, or error code.

6.7 Error Handling

idna_strerror

const char * idna_strerror (*Idna_rc rc*)   [Function]
    rc: an `Idna_rc` return code.

Convert a return code integer to a text string. This string can be used to output a diagnostic message to the user.

IDNA_SUCCESS: Successful operation. This value is guaranteed to always be zero, the remaining ones are only guaranteed to hold non-zero values, for logical comparison purposes.

IDNA_STRINGPREP_ERROR: Error during string preparation.

IDNA_PUNYCODE_ERROR: Error during punycode operation.

IDNA_CONTAINS_NON_LDH: For IDNA_USE_STD3_ASCII_RULES, indicate that the string contains non-LDH ASCII characters.

IDNA_CONTAINS_MINUS: For IDNA_USE_STD3_ASCII_RULES, indicate that the string contains a leading or trailing hyphen-minus (U+002D).

IDNA_INVALID_LENGTH: The final output string is not within the (inclusive) range 1 to 63 characters.

IDNA_NO_ACE_PREFIX: The string does not contain the ACE prefix (for ToUnicode).

IDNA_ROUNDTRIP_VERIFY_ERROR: The ToASCII operation on output string does not equal the input.

IDNA_CONTAINS_ACE_PREFIX: The input contains the ACE prefix (for ToASCII).

IDNA_ICONV_ERROR: Could not convert string in locale encoding.

IDNA_MALLOC_ERROR: Could not allocate buffer (this is typically a fatal error).

IDNA_DLOPEN_ERROR: Could not dlopen the libcidn DSO (only used internally in libc).

Return value: Returns a pointer to a statically allocated string containing a description of the error with the return code `rc` .

7 TLD Functions

Organizations that manage some Top Level Domains (TLDs) have published tables with characters they accept within the domain. The reason may be to reduce complexity that come from using the full Unicode range, and to protect themselves from future (backwards incompatible) changes in the IDN or Unicode specifications. Libidn implement an infrastructure for defining and checking strings against such tables. Libidn also ship some tables from TLDs that we have managed to get permission to use them from. Because these tables are even less static than Unicode or StringPrep tables, it is likely that they will be updated from time to time (even in backwards incompatible ways). The Libidn interface provide a "version" field for each TLD table, which can be compared for equality to guarantee the same operation over time.

From a design point of view, you can regard the TLD tables for IDN as the "localization" step that come after the "internationalization" step provided by the IETF standards.

The TLD functionality rely on up-to-date tables. The latest version of Libidn aim to provide these, but tables with unclear copying conditions, or generally experimental tables, are not included. Some such tables can be found at https://github.com/gnuthor/tldchk.

7.1 Header file tld.h

To use the functions explained in this chapter, you need to include the file tld.h using:

```
#include <tld.h>
```

7.2 Core Functions

tld_check_4t

int tld_check_4t (const uint32_t * in, size_t inlen, size_t * errpos,   [Function]
    const Tld_table * tld)

    in: Array of unicode code points to process. Does not need to be zero terminated.

    inlen: Number of unicode code points.

    errpos: Position of offending character is returned here.

    tld: A Tld_table data structure representing the restrictions for which the input should be tested.

    Test each of the code points in in for whether or not they are allowed by the data structure in tld , return the position of the first character for which this is not the case in errpos .

    Return value: Returns the Tld_rc value TLD_SUCCESS if all code points are valid or when tld is null, TLD_INVALID if a character is not allowed, or additional error codes on general failure conditions.

tld_check_4tz

int tld_check_4tz (const uint32_t * in, size_t * errpos, const   [Function]
    Tld_table * tld)

    in: Zero terminated array of unicode code points to process.

errpos: Position of offending character is returned here.

tld: A `Tld_table` data structure representing the restrictions for which the input should be tested.

Test each of the code points in `in` for whether or not they are allowed by the data structure in `tld` , return the position of the first character for which this is not the case in `errpos` .

Return value: Returns the `Tld_rc` value `TLD_SUCCESS` if all code points are valid or when `tld` is null, `TLD_INVALID` if a character is not allowed, or additional error codes on general failure conditions.

7.3 Utility Functions

tld_get_4

int tld_get_4 (*const uint32_t * in*, *size_t* `inlen`, *char ** out*)   [Function]
    in: Array of unicode code points to process. Does not need to be zero terminated.

    inlen: Number of unicode code points.

    out: Zero terminated ascii result string pointer.

    Isolate the top-level domain of `in` and return it as an ASCII string in `out` .

    Return value: Return `TLD_SUCCESS` on success, or the corresponding `Tld_rc` error code otherwise.

tld_get_4z

int tld_get_4z (*const uint32_t * in*, *char ** out*)   [Function]
    in: Zero terminated array of unicode code points to process.

    out: Zero terminated ascii result string pointer.

    Isolate the top-level domain of `in` and return it as an ASCII string in `out` .

    Return value: Return `TLD_SUCCESS` on success, or the corresponding `Tld_rc` error code otherwise.

tld_get_z

int tld_get_z (*const char * in*, *char ** out*)   [Function]
    in: Zero terminated character array to process.

    out: Zero terminated ascii result string pointer.

    Isolate the top-level domain of `in` and return it as an ASCII string in `out` . The input string `in` may be UTF-8, ISO-8859-1 or any ASCII compatible character encoding.

    Return value: Return `TLD_SUCCESS` on success, or the corresponding `Tld_rc` error code otherwise.

tld_get_table

const Tld_table * tld_get_table (*const char * **tld**, const Tld_table*   [Function]
      *** tables*)

    tld: TLD name (e.g. "com") as zero terminated ASCII byte string.

    tables: Zero terminated array of `Tld_table` info-structures for TLDs.

    Get the TLD table for a named TLD by searching through the given TLD table array.

    Return value: Return structure corresponding to TLD `tld` by going thru `tables` , or return `NULL` if no such structure is found.

tld_default_table

const Tld_table * tld_default_table (*const char * **tld**, const*   [Function]
      *Tld_table ** **overrides**)

    tld: TLD name (e.g. "com") as zero terminated ASCII byte string.

    overrides: Additional zero terminated array of `Tld_table` info-structures for TLDs, or `NULL` to only use library deault tables.

    Get the TLD table for a named TLD, using the internal defaults, possibly overrided by the (optional) supplied tables.

    Return value: Return structure corresponding to TLD `tld_str` , first looking through `overrides` then thru built-in list, or `NULL` if no such structure found.

7.4 High-Level Wrapper Functions

tld_check_4

int tld_check_4 (*const uint32_t * **in**, size_t **inlen**, size_t * **errpos**,*   [Function]
      *const Tld_table ** **overrides**)

    in: Array of unicode code points to process. Does not need to be zero terminated.

    inlen: Number of unicode code points.

    errpos: Position of offending character is returned here.

    overrides: A `Tld_table` array of additional domain restriction structures that complement and supersede the built-in information.

    Test each of the code points in `in` for whether or not they are allowed by the information in `overrides` or by the built-in TLD restriction data. When data for the same TLD is available both internally and in `overrides` , the information in `overrides` takes precedence. If several entries for a specific TLD are found, the first one is used. If `overrides` is `NULL` , only the built-in information is used. The position of the first offending character is returned in `errpos` .

    Return value: Returns the `Tld_rc` value `TLD_SUCCESS` if all code points are valid or when `tld` is null, `TLD_INVALID` if a character is not allowed, or additional error codes on general failure conditions.

tld_check_4z

int **tld_check_4z** (*const uint32_t * in, size_t * errpos, const Tld_table* [Function]
** overrides*)

in: Zero-terminated array of unicode code points to process.

errpos: Position of offending character is returned here.

overrides: A `Tld_table` array of additional domain restriction structures that complement and supersede the built-in information.

Test each of the code points in `in` for whether or not they are allowed by the information in `overrides` or by the built-in TLD restriction data. When data for the same TLD is available both internally and in `overrides` , the information in `overrides` takes precedence. If several entries for a specific TLD are found, the first one is used. If `overrides` is `NULL` , only the built-in information is used. The position of the first offending character is returned in `errpos` .

Return value: Returns the `Tld_rc` value `TLD_SUCCESS` if all code points are valid or when `tld` is null, `TLD_INVALID` if a character is not allowed, or additional error codes on general failure conditions.

tld_check_8z

int **tld_check_8z** (*const char * in, size_t * errpos, const Tld_table *** [Function]
overrides*)

in: Zero-terminated UTF8 string to process.

errpos: Position of offending character is returned here.

overrides: A `Tld_table` array of additional domain restriction structures that complement and supersede the built-in information.

Test each of the characters in `in` for whether or not they are allowed by the information in `overrides` or by the built-in TLD restriction data. When data for the same TLD is available both internally and in `overrides` , the information in `overrides` takes precedence. If several entries for a specific TLD are found, the first one is used. If `overrides` is `NULL` , only the built-in information is used. The position of the first offending character is returned in `errpos` . Note that the error position refers to the decoded character offset rather than the byte position in the string.

Return value: Returns the `Tld_rc` value `TLD_SUCCESS` if all characters are valid or when `tld` is null, `TLD_INVALID` if a character is not allowed, or additional error codes on general failure conditions.

tld_check_lz

int **tld_check_lz** (*const char * in, size_t * errpos, const Tld_table *** [Function]
overrides*)

in: Zero-terminated string in the current locales encoding to process.

errpos: Position of offending character is returned here.

overrides: A `Tld_table` array of additional domain restriction structures that complement and supersede the built-in information.

Test each of the characters in **in** for whether or not they are allowed by the information in **overrides** or by the built-in TLD restriction data. When data for the same TLD is available both internally and in **overrides** , the information in **overrides** takes precedence. If several entries for a specific TLD are found, the first one is used. If **overrides** is **NULL** , only the built-in information is used. The position of the first offending character is returned in **errpos** . Note that the error position refers to the decoded character offset rather than the byte position in the string.

Return value: Returns the `Tld_rc` value `TLD_SUCCESS` if all characters are valid or when `tld` is null, `TLD_INVALID` if a character is not allowed, or additional error codes on general failure conditions.

7.5 Error Handling

tld_strerror

`const char * tld_strerror (Tld_rc rc)`   [Function]

rc: tld return code

Convert a return code integer to a text string. This string can be used to output a diagnostic message to the user.

TLD_SUCCESS: Successful operation. This value is guaranteed to always be zero, the remaining ones are only guaranteed to hold non-zero values, for logical comparison purposes.

TLD_INVALID: Invalid character found.

TLD_NODATA: No input data was provided.

TLD_MALLOC_ERROR: Error during memory allocation.

TLD_ICONV_ERROR: Error during iconv string conversion.

TLD_NO_TLD: No top-level domain found in domain string.

Return value: Returns a pointer to a statically allocated string containing a description of the error with the return code **rc** .

8 PR29 Functions

A deficiency in the specification of Unicode Normalization Forms has been found. The consequence is that some strings can be normalized into different strings by different implementations. In other words, two different implementations may return different output for the same input (because the interpretation of the specification is ambiguous). Further, an implementation invoked again on the one of the output strings may return a different string (because one of the interpretation of the ambiguous specification make normalization non-idempotent). Fortunately, only a select few character sequence exhibit this problem, and none of them are expected to occur in natural languages (due to different linguistic uses of the involved characters).

A full discussion of the problem may be found at:

`http://www.unicode.org/review/pr-29.html`

The PR29 functions below allow you to detect the problem sequence. So when would you want to use these functions? For most applications, such as those using Nameprep for IDN, this is likely only to be an interoperability problem. Thus, you may not want to care about it, as the character sequences will rarely occur naturally. However, if you are using a profile, such as SASLPrep, to process authentication tokens; authorization tokens; or passwords, there is a real danger that attackers may try to use the peculiarities in these strings to attack parts of your system. As only a small number of strings, and no naturally occurring strings, exhibit this problem, the conservative approach of rejecting the strings is recommended. If this approach is not used, you should instead verify that all parts of your system, that process the tokens and passwords, use a NFKC implementation that produce the same output for the same input.

Technically inclined readers may be interested in knowing more about the implementation aspects of the PR29 flaw. See Appendix A [PR29 discussion], page 64.

8.1 Header file `pr29.h`

To use the functions explained in this chapter, you need to include the file **`pr29.h`** using:

```
#include <pr29.h>
```

8.2 Core Functions

pr29_4

`int pr29_4` (*const uint32_t * **in**, size_t **len**)   [Function]
   in: input array with unicode code points.

   len: length of input array with unicode code points.

   Check the input to see if it may be normalized into different strings by different NFKC implementations, due to an anomaly in the NFKC specifications.

   Return value: Returns the **`Pr29_rc`** value **`PR29_SUCCESS`** on success, and **`PR29_PROBLEM`** if the input sequence is a "problem sequence" (i.e., may be normalized into different strings by different implementations).

8.3 Utility Functions

pr29_4z

int pr29_4z (*const uint32_t * in*)   [Function]
> *in*: zero terminated array of Unicode code points.
>
> Check the input to see if it may be normalized into different strings by different NFKC implementations, due to an anomaly in the NFKC specifications.
>
> Return value: Returns the `Pr29_rc` value `PR29_SUCCESS` on success, and `PR29_PROBLEM` if the input sequence is a "problem sequence" (i.e., may be normalized into different strings by different implementations).

pr29_8z

int pr29_8z (*const char * in*)   [Function]
> *in*: zero terminated input UTF-8 string.
>
> Check the input to see if it may be normalized into different strings by different NFKC implementations, due to an anomaly in the NFKC specifications.
>
> Return value: Returns the `Pr29_rc` value `PR29_SUCCESS` on success, and `PR29_PROBLEM` if the input sequence is a "problem sequence" (i.e., may be normalized into different strings by different implementations), or `PR29_STRINGPREP_ERROR` if there was a problem converting the string from UTF-8 to UCS-4.

8.4 Error Handling

pr29_strerror

const char * pr29_strerror (*Pr29_rc rc*)   [Function]
> *rc*: an `Pr29_rc` return code.
>
> Convert a return code integer to a text string. This string can be used to output a diagnostic message to the user.
>
> **PR29_SUCCESS:** Successful operation. This value is guaranteed to always be zero, the remaining ones are only guaranteed to hold non-zero values, for logical comparison purposes.
>
> **PR29_PROBLEM:** A problem sequence was encountered.
>
> **PR29_STRINGPREP_ERROR:** The character set conversion failed (only for `pr29_8z()`).
>
> Return value: Returns a pointer to a statically allocated string containing a description of the error with the return code `rc` .

9 Examples

This chapter contains example code which illustrate how 'Libidn' can be used when writing your own application.

9.1 Example 1

This example demonstrates how the stringprep functions are used.

```
/* example.c --- Example code showing how to use stringprep().
 * Copyright (C) 2002-2015 Simon Josefsson
 *
 * This file is part of GNU Libidn.
 *
 * This program is free software:  you can redistribute it and/or modify
 * it under the terms of the GNU General Public License as published by
 * the Free Software Foundation, either version 3 of the License, or
 * (at your option) any later version.
 *
 * This program is distributed in the hope that it will be useful,
 * but WITHOUT ANY WARRANTY; without even the implied warranty of
 * MERCHANTABILITY or FITNESS FOR A PARTICULAR PURPOSE.  See the
 * GNU General Public License for more details.
 *
 * You should have received a copy of the GNU General Public License
 * along with this program.    If not, see <http://www.gnu.org/licenses/>.
 *
 */


#include <stdio.h>
#include <stdlib.h>
#include <string.h>
#include <locale.h>              /* setlocale() */
#include <stringprep.h>

/*
 * Compiling using libtool and pkg-config is recommended:
 *
 * $ libtool cc -o example example.c `pkg-config --cflags --libs libidn`
 * $ ./example
 * Input string encoded as 'ISO-8859-1':  a
 * Before locale2utf8 (length 2):  aa 0a
 * Before stringprep (length 3):  c2 aa 0a
 * After stringprep (length 2):  61 0a
 * $
 *
 */
```

```
int
main (void)
{
  char buf[BUFSIZ];
  char *p;
  int rc;
  size_t i;

  setlocale (LC_ALL, "");

  printf ("Input string encoded as '%s':  ", stringprep_locale_charset ());
  fflush (stdout);
  if (!fgets (buf, BUFSIZ, stdin))
    perror ("fgets");
  buf[strlen (buf) - 1] = '\0';

  printf ("Before locale2utf8 (length %ld):  ", (long int) strlen (buf));
  for (i = 0; i < strlen (buf); i++)
    printf ("%02x ", buf[i] & 0xFF);
  printf ("\n");

  p = stringprep_locale_to_utf8 (buf);
  if (p)
    {
      strcpy (buf, p);
      free (p);
    }
  else
    printf ("Could not convert string to UTF-8, continuing anyway...\n");

  printf ("Before stringprep (length %ld):  ", (long int) strlen (buf));
  for (i = 0; i < strlen (buf); i++)
    printf ("%02x ", buf[i] & 0xFF);
  printf ("\n");

  rc = stringprep (buf, BUFSIZ, 0, stringprep_nameprep);
  if (rc != STRINGPREP_OK)
    printf ("Stringprep failed (%d):  %s\n", rc, stringprep_strerror (rc));
  else
    {
      printf ("After stringprep (length %ld):  ", (long int) strlen (buf));
      for (i = 0; i < strlen (buf); i++)
        printf ("%02x ", buf[i] & 0xFF);
      printf ("\n");
    }

  return 0;
```

```
}
```

9.2 Example 2

This example demonstrates how the punycode functions are used.

```
/* example2.c --- Example code showing how to use punycode.
 * Copyright (C) 2002-2015 Simon Josefsson
 * Copyright (C) 2002  Adam M. Costello
 *
 * This file is part of GNU Libidn.
 *
 * This program is free software:  you can redistribute it and/or modify
 * it under the terms of the GNU General Public License as published by
 * the Free Software Foundation, either version 3 of the License, or
 * (at your option) any later version.
 *
 * This program is distributed in the hope that it will be useful,
 * but WITHOUT ANY WARRANTY; without even the implied warranty of
 * MERCHANTABILITY or FITNESS FOR A PARTICULAR PURPOSE.  See the
 * GNU General Public License for more details.
 *
 * You should have received a copy of the GNU General Public License
 * along with this program.   If not, see <http://www.gnu.org/licenses/>.
 *
 */

#include <locale.h>              /* setlocale() */

/*
 * This file is derived from RFC 3492 written by Adam M. Costello.
 *
 * Disclaimer and license:  Regarding this entire document or any
 * portion of it (including the pseudocode and C code), the author
 * makes no guarantees and is not responsible for any damage resulting
 * from its use.   The author grants irrevocable permission to anyone
 * to use, modify, and distribute it in any way that does not diminish
 * the rights of anyone else to use, modify, and distribute it,
 * provided that redistributed derivative works do not contain
 * misleading author or version information.   Derivative works need
 * not be licensed under similar terms.
 *
 */

#include <assert.h>
#include <stdio.h>
#include <stdlib.h>
#include <string.h>
```

```
#include <punycode.h>

/* For testing, we'll just set some compile-time limits rather than */
/* use malloc(), and set a compile-time option rather than using a  */
/* command-line option.

enum
{
  unicode_max_length = 256,
  ace_max_length = 256
};

static void
usage (char **argv)
{
  fprintf (stderr,
           "\n"
           "%s -e reads code points and writes a Punycode string.\n"
           "%s -d reads a Punycode string and writes code points.\n"
           "\n"
           "Input and output are plain text in the native character set.\n"
           "Code points are in the form u+hex separated by whitespace.\n"
           "Although the specification allows Punycode strings to contain\n"
           "any characters from the ASCII repertoire, this test code\n"
           "supports only the printable characters, and needs the Punycode\n"
           "string to be followed by a newline.\n"
           "The case of the u in u+hex is the force-to-uppercase flag.\n",
           argv[0], argv[0]);
  exit (EXIT_FAILURE);
}

static void
fail (const char *msg)
{
  fputs (msg, stderr);
  exit (EXIT_FAILURE);
}

static const char too_big[] =
  "input or output is too large, recompile with larger limits\n";
static const char invalid_input[] = "invalid input\n";
static const char overflow[] = "arithmetic overflow\n";
static const char io_error[] = "I/O error\n";

/* The following string is used to convert printable */
/* characters between ASCII and the native charset:   */
```

```c
static const char print_ascii[] = "\n\n\n\n\n\n\n\n\n\n\n\n\n\n\n\n" "\n\n\n\n\n\n\n\n\n\n\
  "ABCDEFGHIJKLMNO"
  "PQRSTUVWXYZ[\\]^_" "`abcdefghijklmno" "pqrstuvwxyz{|}~\n";

int
main (int argc, char **argv)
{
  enum punycode_status status;
  int r;
  size_t input_length, output_length, j;
  unsigned char case_flags[unicode_max_length];

  setlocale (LC_ALL, "");

  if (argc != 2)
    usage (argv);
  if (argv[1][0] != '-')
    usage (argv);
  if (argv[1][2] != 0)
    usage (argv);

  if (argv[1][1] == 'e')
    {
      uint32_t input[unicode_max_length];
      unsigned long codept;
      char output[ace_max_length + 1], uplus[3];
      int c;

      /* Read the input code points:  */

      input_length = 0;

      for (;;)
        {
          r = scanf ("%2s%lx", uplus, &codept);
          if (ferror (stdin))
            fail (io_error);
          if (r == EOF || r == 0)
            break;

          if (r != 2 || uplus[1] != '+' || codept > (uint32_t) - 1)
            {
              fail (invalid_input);
            }

          if (input_length == unicode_max_length)
```

```
        fail (too_big);

      if (uplus[0] == 'u')
        case_flags[input_length] = 0;
      else if (uplus[0] == 'U')
        case_flags[input_length] = 1;
      else
        fail (invalid_input);

      input[input_length++] = codept;
    }

  /* Encode:  */

  output_length = ace_max_length;
  status = punycode_encode (input_length, input, case_flags,
                            &output_length, output);
  if (status == punycode_bad_input)
    fail (invalid_input);
  if (status == punycode_big_output)
    fail (too_big);
  if (status == punycode_overflow)
    fail (overflow);
  assert (status == punycode_success);

  /* Convert to native charset and output:  */

  for (j = 0; j < output_length; ++j)
    {
      c = output[j];
      assert (c >= 0 && c <= 127);
      if (print_ascii[c] == 0)
        fail (invalid_input);
      output[j] = print_ascii[c];
    }

  output[j] = 0;
  r = puts (output);
  if (r == EOF)
    fail (io_error);
  return EXIT_SUCCESS;
}

if (argv[1][1] == 'd')
  {
    char input[ace_max_length + 2], *p, *pp;
    uint32_t output[unicode_max_length];
```

```
/* Read the Punycode input string and convert to ASCII: */

if (!fgets (input, ace_max_length + 2, stdin))
  fail (io_error);
if (ferror (stdin))
  fail (io_error);
if (feof (stdin))
  fail (invalid_input);
input_length = strlen (input) - 1;
if (input[input_length] != '\n')
  fail (too_big);
input[input_length] = 0;

for (p = input; *p != 0; ++p)
  {
    pp = strchr (print_ascii, *p);
    if (pp == 0)
      fail (invalid_input);
    *p = pp - print_ascii;
  }

/* Decode:  */

output_length = unicode_max_length;
status = punycode_decode (input_length, input, &output_length,
                          output, case_flags);
if (status == punycode_bad_input)
  fail (invalid_input);
if (status == punycode_big_output)
  fail (too_big);
if (status == punycode_overflow)
  fail (overflow);
assert (status == punycode_success);

/* Output the result:  */

for (j = 0; j < output_length; ++j)
  {
    r = printf ("%s+%04lX\n",
                case_flags[j] ? "U" :  "u", (unsigned long) output[j]);
    if (r < 0)
      fail (io_error);
  }

  return EXIT_SUCCESS;
}
```

```
    usage (argv);
    return EXIT_SUCCESS;            /* not reached, but quiets compiler warning */
}
```

9.3 Example 3

This example demonstrates how the library is used to convert internationalized domain names into ASCII compatible names.

```
/* example3.c --- Example ToASCII() code showing how to use Libidn.
 * Copyright (C) 2002-2015 Simon Josefsson
 *
 * This file is part of GNU Libidn.
 *
 * This program is free software:  you can redistribute it and/or modify
 * it under the terms of the GNU General Public License as published by
 * the Free Software Foundation, either version 3 of the License, or
 * (at your option) any later version.
 *
 * This program is distributed in the hope that it will be useful,
 * but WITHOUT ANY WARRANTY; without even the implied warranty of
 * MERCHANTABILITY or FITNESS FOR A PARTICULAR PURPOSE.  See the
 * GNU General Public License for more details.
 *
 * You should have received a copy of the GNU General Public License
 * along with this program.   If not, see <http://www.gnu.org/licenses/>.
 *
 */


#include <stdio.h>
#include <stdlib.h>
#include <string.h>
#include <locale.h>            /* setlocale() */
#include <stringprep.h>        /* stringprep_locale_charset() */
#include <idna.h>             /* idna_to_ascii_lz() */

/*
 * Compiling using libtool and pkg-config is recommended:
 *
 * $ libtool cc -o example3 example3.c `pkg-config --cflags --libs libidn`
 * $ ./example3
 * Input domain encoded as 'ISO-8859-1':  www.raksmorgaasa.example
 * Read string (length 23):  77 77 77 2e 72 e4 6b 73 6d f6 72 67 e5 73 aa 2e 65 78 61 ̶
 * ACE label (length 33):  'www.xn--rksmrgsa-0zap8p.example'
 * 77 77 77 2e 78 6e 2d 2d 72 6b 73 6d 72 67 73 61 2d 30 7a 61 70 38 70 2e 65 78 61 6d
 * $
 *
```

```
*/

int
main (void)
{
  char buf[BUFSIZ];
  char *p;
  int rc;
  size_t i;

  setlocale (LC_ALL, "");

  printf ("Input domain encoded as '%s': ", stringprep_locale_charset ());
  fflush (stdout);
  if (!fgets (buf, BUFSIZ, stdin))
    perror ("fgets");
  buf[strlen (buf) - 1] = '\0';

  printf ("Read string (length %ld): ", (long int) strlen (buf));
  for (i = 0; i < strlen (buf); i++)
    printf ("%02x ", buf[i] & 0xFF);
  printf ("\n");

  rc = idna_to_ascii_lz (buf, &p, 0);
  if (rc != IDNA_SUCCESS)
    {
      printf ("ToASCII() failed (%d): %s\n", rc, idna_strerror (rc));
      return EXIT_FAILURE;
    }

  printf ("ACE label (length %ld): '%s'\n", (long int) strlen (p), p);
  for (i = 0; i < strlen (p); i++)
    printf ("%02x ", p[i] & 0xFF);
  printf ("\n");

  free (p);

  return 0;
}
```

9.4 Example 4

This example demonstrates how the library is used to convert ASCII compatible names to internationalized domain names.

```
/* example4.c --- Example ToUnicode() code showing how to use Libidn.
 * Copyright (C) 2002-2015 Simon Josefsson
 *
```

```
 * This file is part of GNU Libidn.
 *
 * This program is free software:  you can redistribute it and/or modify
 * it under the terms of the GNU General Public License as published by
 * the Free Software Foundation, either version 3 of the License, or
 * (at your option) any later version.
 *
 * This program is distributed in the hope that it will be useful,
 * but WITHOUT ANY WARRANTY; without even the implied warranty of
 * MERCHANTABILITY or FITNESS FOR A PARTICULAR PURPOSE.  See the
 * GNU General Public License for more details.
 *
 * You should have received a copy of the GNU General Public License
 * along with this program.    If not, see <http://www.gnu.org/licenses/>.
 *
 */

#include <stdio.h>
#include <stdlib.h>
#include <string.h>
#include <locale.h>               /* setlocale() */
#include <stringprep.h>           /* stringprep_locale_charset() */
#include <idna.h>                 /* idna_to_unicode_lzlz() */

/*
 * Compiling using libtool and pkg-config is recommended:
 *
 * $ libtool cc -o example4 example4.c `pkg-config --cflags --libs libidn`
 * $ ./example4
 * Input domain encoded as 'ISO-8859-1':  www.xn--rksmrgsa-0zap8p.example
 * Read string (length 33):  77 77 77 2e 78 6e 2d 2d 72 6b 73 6d 72 67 73 61 2d 30 7a 6
 * ACE label (length 23):  'www.raksmorgaasa.example'
 * 77 77 77 2e 72 e4 6b 73 6d f6 72 67 e5 73 61 2e 65 78 61 6d 70 6c 65
 * $
 *
 */

int
main (void)
{
  char buf[BUFSIZ];
  char *p;
  int rc;
  size_t i;

  setlocale (LC_ALL, "");
```

```
   printf ("Input domain encoded as '%s':  ", stringprep_locale_charset ());
   fflush (stdout);
   if (!fgets (buf, BUFSIZ, stdin))
     perror ("fgets");
   buf[strlen (buf) - 1] = '\0';

   printf ("Read string (length %ld):  ", (long int) strlen (buf));
   for (i = 0; i < strlen (buf); i++)
     printf ("%02x ", buf[i] & 0xFF);
   printf ("\n");

   rc = idna_to_unicode_lzlz (buf, &p, 0);
   if (rc != IDNA_SUCCESS)
     {
       printf ("ToUnicode() failed (%d):  %s\n", rc, idna_strerror (rc));
       return EXIT_FAILURE;
     }

   printf ("ACE label (length %ld):  '%s'\n", (long int) strlen (p), p);
   for (i = 0; i < strlen (p); i++)
     printf ("%02x ", p[i] & 0xFF);
   printf ("\n");

   free (p);

   return 0;
}
```

9.5 Example 5

This example demonstrates how the library is used to check a string for invalid characters within a specific TLD.

```
/* example5.c --- Example TLD checking.
 * Copyright (C) 2004-2015 Simon Josefsson
 *
 * This file is part of GNU Libidn.
 *
 * This program is free software:  you can redistribute it and/or modify
 * it under the terms of the GNU General Public License as published by
 * the Free Software Foundation, either version 3 of the License, or
 * (at your option) any later version.
 *
 * This program is distributed in the hope that it will be useful,
 * but WITHOUT ANY WARRANTY; without even the implied warranty of
 * MERCHANTABILITY or FITNESS FOR A PARTICULAR PURPOSE.  See the
 * GNU General Public License for more details.
 *
```

```
 * You should have received a copy of the GNU General Public License
 * along with this program.    If not, see <http://www.gnu.org/licenses/>.
 *
 */


#include <stdio.h>
#include <stdlib.h>
#include <string.h>

/* Get stringprep_locale_charset, etc.  */
#include <stringprep.h>

/* Get idna_to_ascii_8z, etc.  */
#include <idna.h>

/* Get tld_check_4z.  */
#include <tld.h>

/*
 * Compiling using libtool and pkg-config is recommended:
 *
 * $ libtool cc -o example5 example5.c `pkg-config --cflags --libs libidn`
 * $ ./example5
 * Input domain encoded as 'UTF-8':  fooss.no
 * Read string (length 8):   66 6f 6f c3 9f 2e 6e 6f
 * ToASCII string (length 8):  fooss.no
 * ToUnicode string:   U+0066 U+006f U+006f U+0073 U+0073 U+002e U+006e U+006f
 * Domain accepted by TLD check
 *
 * $ ./example5
 * Input domain encoded as 'UTF-8':  greuroeuron.no
 * Read string (length 12):   67 72 e2 82 ac e2 82 ac 6e 2e 6e 6f
 * ToASCII string (length 16):  xn--grn-150aa.no
 * ToUnicode string:   U+0067 U+0072 U+20ac U+20ac U+006e U+002e U+006e U+006f
 * Domain rejected by TLD check, Unicode position 2
 *
 */

int
main (void)
{
  char buf[BUFSIZ];
  char *p;
  uint32_t *r;
  int rc;
  size_t errpos, i;
```

```
printf ("Input domain encoded as '%s': ", stringprep_locale_charset ());
fflush (stdout);
if (!fgets (buf, BUFSIZ, stdin))
  perror ("fgets");
buf[strlen (buf) - 1] = '\0';

printf ("Read string (length %ld): ", (long int) strlen (buf));
for (i = 0; i < strlen (buf); i++)
  printf ("%02x ", buf[i] & 0xFF);
printf ("\n");

p = stringprep_locale_to_utf8 (buf);
if (p)
  {
    strcpy (buf, p);
    free (p);
  }
else
  printf ("Could not convert string to UTF-8, continuing anyway...\n");

rc = idna_to_ascii_8z (buf, &p, 0);
if (rc != IDNA_SUCCESS)
  {
    printf ("idna_to_ascii_8z failed (%d): %s\n", rc, idna_strerror (rc));
    return 2;
  }

printf ("ToASCII string (length %ld): %s\n", (long int) strlen (p), p);

rc = idna_to_unicode_8z4z (p, &r, 0);
free (p);
if (rc != IDNA_SUCCESS)
  {
    printf ("idna_to_unicode_8z4z failed (%d): %s\n",
            rc, idna_strerror (rc));
    return 2;
  }

printf ("ToUnicode string: ");
for (i = 0; r[i]; i++)
  printf ("U+%04x ", r[i]);
printf ("\n");

rc = tld_check_4z (r, &errpos, NULL);
free (r);
if (rc == TLD_INVALID)
  {
```

```
        printf ("Domain rejected by TLD check, Unicode position %ld\n", (long int) errpos
        return 1;
    }
  else if (rc != TLD_SUCCESS)
    {
      printf ("tld_check_4z() failed (%d):  %s\n", rc, tld_strerror (rc));
      return 2;
    }

  printf ("Domain accepted by TLD check\n");

  return 0;
}
```

10 Invoking idn

10.1 Name

GNU Libidn (idn) – Internationalized Domain Names command line tool

10.2 Description

idn allows internationalized string preparation ('**stringprep**'), encoding and decoding of punycode data, and IDNA ToASCII/ToUnicode operations to be performed on the command line.

If strings are specified on the command line, they are used as input and the computed output is printed to standard output **stdout**. If no strings are specified on the command line, the program read data, line by line, from the standard input **stdin**, and print the computed output to standard output. What processing is performed (e.g., ToASCII, or Punycode encode) is indicated by options. If any errors are encountered, the execution of the applications is aborted.

All strings are expected to be encoded in the preferred charset used by your locale. Use **--debug** to find out what this charset is. You can override the charset used by setting environment variable **CHARSET**.

To process a string that starts with -, for example -foo, use -- to signal the end of parameters, as in idn --quiet -a -- -foo.

10.3 Options

idn recognizes these commands:

```
    -h, --help              Print help and exit

    -V, --version           Print version and exit

    -s, --stringprep        Prepare string according to nameprep profile

    -d, --punycode-decode   Decode Punycode

    -e, --punycode-encode   Encode Punycode

    -a, --idna-to-ascii     Convert to ACE according to IDNA (default mode)

    -u, --idna-to-unicode   Convert from ACE according to IDNA

        --allow-unassigned  Toggle IDNA AllowUnassigned flag (default off)

        --usestd3asciirules Toggle IDNA UseSTD3ASCIIRules flag (default off)

        --no-tld            Don't check string for TLD specific rules
                            Only for --idna-to-ascii and --idna-to-unicode
```

```
-n, --nfkc                  Normalize string according to Unicode v3.2 NFKC

-p, --profile=STRING        Use specified stringprep profile instead
                               Valid stringprep profiles: 'Nameprep',
                               'iSCSI', 'Nodeprep', 'Resourceprep',
                               'trace', 'SASLprep'

   --debug                  Print debugging information

   --quiet                  Silent operation
```

10.4 Environment Variables

The *CHARSET* environment variable can be used to override what character set to be used for decoding incoming data (i.e., on the command line or on the standard input stream), and to encode data to the standard output. If your system is set up correctly, however, the application will guess which character set is used automatically. Example usage:

```
$ CHARSET=ISO-8859-1 idn --punycode-encode
...
```

10.5 Examples

Standard usage, reading input from standard input:

```
jas@latte:~$ idn
libidn 0.3.5
Copyright 2002, 2003 Simon Josefsson.
GNU Libidn comes with NO WARRANTY, to the extent permitted by law.
You may redistribute copies of GNU Libidn under the terms of
the GNU Lesser General Public License.  For more information
about these matters, see the file named COPYING.LIB.
Type each input string on a line by itself, terminated by a newline character.
räksmörgås.se
xn--rksmrgs-5wao1o.se
jas@latte:~$
```

Reading input from command line, and disable printing copyright and license information:

```
jas@latte:~$ idn --quiet räksmörgås.se blåbærgrød.no
xn--rksmrgs-5wao1o.se
xn--blbrgrd-fxak7p.no
jas@latte:~$
```

Accessing a specific StringPrep profile directly:

```
jas@latte:~$ idn --quiet --profile=SASLprep --stringprep teßt[a]
teßta
jas@latte:~$
```

10.6 Troubleshooting

Getting character data encoded right, and making sure Libidn use the same encoding, can be difficult. The reason for this is that most systems encode character data in more than one character encoding, i.e., using UTF-8 together with ISO-8859-1 or ISO-2022-JP. This problem is likely to continue to exist until only one character encoding come out as the evolutionary winner, or (more likely, at least to some extents) forever.

The first step to troubleshooting character encoding problems with Libidn is to use the '--debug' parameter to find out which character set encoding 'idn' believe your locale uses.

```
jas@latte:~$ idn --debug --quiet ""
system locale uses charset 'UTF-8'.

jas@latte:~$
```

If it prints ANSI_X3.4-1968 (i.e., US-ASCII), this indicate you have not configured your locale properly. To configure the locale, you can, for example, use 'LANG=sv_SE.UTF-8; export LANG' at a /bin/sh prompt, to set up your locale for a Swedish environment using UTF-8 as the encoding.

Sometimes 'idn' appear to be unable to translate from your system locale into UTF-8 (which is used internally), and you get an error like the following:

```
jas@latte:~$ idn --quiet foo
idn: could not convert from ISO-8859-1 to UTF-8.
jas@latte:~$
```

The simplest explanation is that you haven't installed the 'iconv' conversion tools. You can find it as a standalone library in GNU Libiconv (http://www.gnu.org/software/libiconv/). On many GNU/Linux systems, this library is part of the system, but you may have to install additional packages (e.g., 'glibc-locale' for Debian) to be able to use it.

Another explanation is that the error is correct and you are feeding 'idn' invalid data. This can happen inadvertently if you are not careful with the character set encoding you use. For example, if your shell run in a ISO-8859-1 environment, and you invoke 'idn' with the 'CHARSET' environment variable as follows, you will feed it ISO-8859-1 characters but force it to believe they are UTF-8. Naturally this will lead to an error, unless the byte sequences happen to be valid UTF-8. Note that even if you don't get an error, the output may be incorrect in this situation, because ISO-8859-1 and UTF-8 does not in general encode the same characters as the same byte sequences.

```
jas@latte:~$ idn --quiet --debug ""
system locale uses charset 'ISO-8859-1'.

jas@latte:~$ CHARSET=UTF-8 idn --quiet --debug räksmörgås
system locale uses charset 'UTF-8'.
input[0] = U+0072
input[1] = U+4af3
input[2] = U+006d
input[3] = U+1b29e5
input[4] = U+0073
output[0] = U+0078
output[1] = U+006e
```

```
output[2]  = U+002d
output[3]  = U+002d
output[4]  = U+0072
output[5]  = U+006d
output[6]  = U+0073
output[7]  = U+002d
output[8]  = U+0068
output[9]  = U+0069
output[10] = U+0036
output[11] = U+0064
output[12] = U+0035
output[13] = U+0039
output[14] = U+0037
output[15] = U+0035
output[16] = U+0035
output[17] = U+0032
output[18] = U+0061
xn--rms-hi6d597552a
jas@latte:~$
```

The sense moral here is to forget about 'CHARSET' (configure your locales properly instead) unless you know what you are doing, and if you want to use it, do it carefully, after verifying with '--debug' that you get the desired results.

11 Emacs API

Included in Libidn are `punycode.el` and `idna.el` that provides an Emacs Lisp API to (a limited set of) the Libidn API. This section describes the API. Currently the IDNA API always set the `UseSTD3ASCIIRules` flag and clear the `AllowUnassigned` flag, in the future there may be functionality to specify these flags via the API.

11.1 Punycode Emacs API

`punycode-program`   [Variable]
> Name of the GNU Libidn `idn` application. The default is 'idn'. This variable can be customized.

`punycode-environment`   [Variable]
> List of environment variable definitions prepended to 'process-environment'. The default is '("CHARSET=UTF-8")'. This variable can be customized.

`punycode-encode-parameters`   [Variable]
> List of parameters passed to *punycode-program* to invoke punycode encoding mode. The default is '("--quiet" "--punycode-encode")'. This variable can be customized.

`punycode-decode-parameters`   [Variable]
> Parameters passed to *punycode-program* to invoke punycode decoding mode. The default is '("--quiet" "--punycode-decode")'. This variable can be customized.

`punycode-encode` *string*   [Function]
> Returns a Punycode encoding of the *string*, after converting the input into UTF-8.

`punycode-decode` *string*   [Function]
> Returns a possibly multibyte string which is the decoding of the *string* which is a punycode encoded string.

11.2 IDNA Emacs API

`idna-program`   [Variable]
> Name of the GNU Libidn `idn` application. The default is 'idn'. This variable can be customized.

`idna-environment`   [Variable]
> List of environment variable definitions prepended to 'process-environment'. The default is '("CHARSET=UTF-8")'. This variable can be customized.

`idna-to-ascii-parameters`   [Variable]
> List of parameters passed to *idna-program* to invoke IDNA ToASCII mode. The default is '("--quiet" "--idna-to-ascii" "--usestd3asciirules")'. This variable can be customized.

idna-to-unicode-parameters   [Variable]

    Parameters passed *idna-program* to invoke IDNA ToUnicode mode. The default is
    `("--quiet" "--idna-to-unicode" "--usestd3asciirules")`'. This variable can
    be customized.

idna-to-ascii *string*   [Function]

    Returns an ASCII Compatible Encoding (ACE) of the string computed by the IDNA
    ToASCII operation on the input *string*, after converting the input to UTF-8.

idna-to-unicode *string*   [Function]

    Returns a possibly multibyte string which is the output of the IDNA ToUnicode
    operation computed on the input *string*.

12 Java API

Libidn has been ported to the Java programming language, and as a consequence most of the API is available to native Java applications. This section contain notes on this support, complete documentation is pending.

The Java library, if Libidn has been built with Java support (see Section 1.7 [Downloading and Installing], page 6), will be placed in `java/libidn-1.32.jar`. The source code is below `java/` in Maven directory layout, and there is a Maven `pom.xml` build script as well. Source code files are in `java/src/main/java/gnu/inet/encoding/`.

12.1 Overview

This package provides a Java implementation of the Internationalized Domain Names in Applications (IDNA) standard. It is written entirely in Java and does not require any additional libraries to be set up.

The gnu.inet.encoding.IDNA class offers two public functions, toASCII and toUnicode which can be used as follows:

```
gnu.inet.encoding.IDNA.toASCII("blöds.züg");
gnu.inet.encoding.IDNA.toUnicode("xn--blds-6qa.xn--zg-xka");
```

12.2 Miscellaneous Programs

The `java/src/util/java/` directory contains several programs that are related to the Java part of GNU Libidn, but that don't need to be included in the main source tree or the JAR file.

12.2.1 GenerateRFC3454

This program parses RFC3454 and creates the RFC3454.java program that is required during the StringPrep phase.

The RFC can be found at various locations, for example at http://www.ietf.org/rfc/rfc3454.txt.

Invoke the program as follows:

```
$ java GenerateRFC3454
Creating RFC3454.java... Ok.
```

12.2.2 GenerateNFKC

The GenerateNFKC program parses the Unicode character database file and generates all the tables required for NFKC. This program requires the two files UnicodeData.txt and CompositionExclusions.txt of version 3.2 of the Unicode files. Note that RFC3454 (Stringprep) defines that Unicode version 3.2 is to be used, not the latest version.

The Unicode data files can be found at http://www.unicode.org/Public/.

Invoke the program as follows:

```
$ java GenerateNFKC
Creating CombiningClass.java... Ok.
Creating DecompositionKeys.java... Ok.
Creating DecompositionMappings.java... Ok.
Creating Composition.java... Ok.
```

12.2.3 TestIDNA

The TestIDNA program allows to test the IDNA implementation manually or against Simon Josefsson's test vectors.

The test vectors can be found at the Libidn homepage, `http://www.gnu.org/software/libidn/`.

To test the transformation manually, use:

```
$ java -cp .:/usr/share/java/libidn.jar TestIDNA -a <string to test>
Input: <string to test>
Output: <toASCII(string to test)>
$ java -cp .:/usr/share/java/libidn.jar TestIDNA -u <string to test>
Input: <string to test>
Output: <toUnicode(string to test)>
```

To test against draft-josefsson-idn-test-vectors.html, use:

```
$ java -cp .:/usr/share/java/libidn/libidn.jar TestIDNA -t
No errors detected!
```

12.2.4 TestNFKC

The TestNFKC program allows to test the NFKC implementation manually or against the NormalizationTest.txt file from the Unicode data files.

To test the normalization manually, use:

```
$ java -cp .:/usr/share/java/libidn.jar TestNFKC <string to test>
Input: <string to test>
Output: <nfkc version of the string to test>
```

To test against NormalizationTest.txt:

```
$ java -cp .:/usr/share/java/libidn.jar TestNFKC
No errors detected!
```

12.3 Possible Problems

Beware of Bugs: This Java API needs a lot more testing, especially with "exotic" character sets. While it works for me, it may not work for you.

Encoding of your Java sources: If you are using non-ASCII characters in your Java source code, make sure javac compiles your programs with the correct encoding. If necessary specify the encoding using the -encoding parameter.

Java Unicode handling: Java 1.4 only handles 16-bit Unicode code points (i.e. characters in the Basic Multilingual Plane), this implementation therefore ignores all references to so-called Supplementary Characters (U+10000 to U+10FFFF). Starting from Java 1.5, these characters will also be supported by Java, but this will require changes to this library. See also the next section.

12.4 A Note on Java and Unicode

This library uses Java's built-in 'char' datatype. Up to Java 1.4, this datatype only supports 16-bit Unicode code points, also called the Basic Multilingual Plane. For this reason, this library doesn't work for Supplementary Characters (i.e. characters from U+10000 to U+10FFFF). All references to such characters are silently ignored.

Starting from Java 1.5, also Supplementary Characters will be supported. However, this will require changes in the present version of the library. Java 1.5 is currently in beta status.

For more information refer to the documentation of java.lang.Character in the JDK API.

13 C# API

The Libidn library has been ported to the C# language. The port reside in the top-level **csharp/** directory. Currently, no further documentation about the implementation or the API is available. However, the C# port was based on the Java port, and the API is exactly the same as in the Java version. The help files for the Java API may thus be useful.

14 Acknowledgements

The punycode implementation was taken from the IETF IDN Punycode specification, by Adam M. Costello. The TLD code was contributed by Thomas Jacob. The Java implementation was contributed by Oliver Hitz. The C# implementation was contributed by Alexander Gnauck. The Unicode tables were provided by Unicode, Inc. Some functions for dealing with Unicode (see nfkc.c and toutf8.c) were borrowed from GLib, downloaded from `http://www.gtk.org/`. The manual borrowed text from Libgcrypt by Werner Koch.

Inspiration for many things that, consciously or not, have gone into this package is due to a number of free software package that the author has been exposed to. The author wishes to acknowledge the free software community in general, for giving an example on what role software development can play in the modern society.

Several people reported bugs, sent patches or suggested improvements, see the file THANKS in the top-level directory of the source code.

15 History

The complete history of user visible changes is stored in the file NEWS in the top-level directory of the source code tree. The complete history of modifications to each file is stored in the file ChangeLog in the same directory. This section contain a condensed version of that information, in the form of "milestones" for the project.

Stringprep implementation.
        Version 0.0.0 released on 2002-11-05.

IDNA and Punycode implementations, part of the GNU project.
        Version 0.1.0 released on 2003-01-05.

Uses official IDNA ACE prefix xn--.
        Version 0.1.7 released on 2003-02-12.

Command line interface.
        Version 0.1.11 released on 2003-02-26.

GNU Libc add-on proposed.
        Version 0.1.12 released on 2003-03-06.

Interoperability testing during IDNConnect.
        Version 0.3.1 released on 2003-10-02.

TLD restriction testing.
        Version 0.4.0 released on 2004-02-28.

GNU Libc add-on integrated.
        Version 0.4.1 released on 2004-03-08.

Native Java implementation.
        Version 0.4.2-0.4.9 released between 2004-03-20 and 2004-06-11.

PR-29 functions for "problem sequences".
        Version 0.5.0 released on 2004-06-26.

Many small portability fixes and wider use.
        Version 0.5.1 through 0.5.20, released between 2004-07-09 and 2005-10-23.

Native C# implementation.
        Version 0.6.0 released on 2005-12-03.

Windows support through cross-compilation.
        Version 0.6.1 released on 2006-01-20.

Library declared stable by releasing v1.0.
        Version 1.0 released on 2007-07-31.

Appendix A PR29 discussion

If you wish to experiment with a modified Unicode NFKC implementation according to the PR29 proposal, you may find the following bug report useful. However, I have not verified that the suggested modifications are correct. For reference, I'm including my response to the report as well.

```
From: Rick McGowan <rick@unicode.org>
Subject: Possible bug and status of PR 29 change(s)
To: bug-libidn@gnu.org
Date: Wed, 27 Oct 2004 14:49:17 -0700


Hello. On behalf of the Unicode Consortium editorial committee, I would
like to find out more information about the PR 29 fixes, if any, and
functions in Libidn. Your implementation was listed in the text of PR29 as
needing investigation, so I am following up on several implementations.

The UTC has accepted the proposed fix to D2 as outlined in PR29, and a new
draft of UAX #15 has been issued.

I have looked at Libidn 0.5.8 (today), and there may still be a possible
bug in NFKC.java and nfkc.c.


------------------------------------------------------


1. In NFKC.java, this line in canonicalOrdering():

      if (i > 0 && (last_cc == 0 || last_cc != cc)) {

should perhaps be changed to:

      if (i > 0 && (last_cc == 0 || last_cc < cc)) {

but I'm not sure of the sense of this comparison.


------------------------------------------------------


2. In nfkc.c, function _g_utf8_normalize_wc() has this code:

        if (i > 0 &&
            (last_cc == 0 || last_cc != cc) &&
            combine (wc_buffer[last_start], wc_buffer[i],
                    &wc_buffer[last_start]))
          {

This appears to have the same bug as the current Python implementation (in
Python 2.3.4). The code should be checking, as per new rule D2 UAX #15
update, that the next combining character is the same or HIGHER than the
```

current one. It now checks to see if it's non-zero and not equal.

The above line(s) should perhaps be changed to:

```
        if (i > 0 &&
            (last_cc == 0 || last_cc < cc) &&
            combine (wc_buffer[last_start], wc_buffer[i],
                    &wc_buffer[last_start]))
          {
```

but I'm not sure of the sense of the comparison (< or > or <=?) here.

In the text of PR29, I will be marking Libidn as "needs change" and adding
the version number that I checked. If any further change is made, please
let me know the release version, and I'll update again.

Regards,
        Rick McGowan

From: Simon Josefsson <jas@extundo.com>
Subject: Re: Possible bug and status of PR 29 change(s)
To: Rick McGowan <rick@unicode.org>
Cc: bug-libidn@gnu.org
Date: Thu, 28 Oct 2004 09:47:47 +0200

Rick McGowan <rick@unicode.org> writes:

> Hello. On behalf of the Unicode Consortium editorial committee, I would
> like to find out more information about the PR 29 fixes, if any, and
> functions in Libidn. Your implementation was listed in the text of PR29 as
> needing investigation, so I am following up on several implementations.
>
> The UTC has accepted the proposed fix to D2 as outlined in PR29, and a new
> draft of UAX #15 has been issued.
>
> I have looked at Libidn 0.5.8 (today), and there may still be a possible
> bug in NFKC.java and nfkc.c.

Hello Rick.

I believe the current behavior is intentional. Libidn do not aim to
implement latest-and-greatest NFKC, it aim to implement the NFKC
functionality required for StringPrep and IDN. As you may know,
StringPrep/IDN reference Unicode 3.2.0, and explicitly says any later
changes (which I consider PR29 as) do not apply.

In fact, I believe that would I incorporate the changes suggested in

PR29, I would in fact be violating the IDN specifications.

Thanks for looking into the code and finding the place where the
change could be made. I'll see if I can mention this in the manual
somewhere, for technically interested readers.

Regards,
Simon

Appendix B On Label Separators

Some strings contains characters whose NFKC normalized form contain the ASCII dot (0x2E, "."). Examples of these characters are U+2024 (ONE DOT LEADER) and U+248C (DIGIT FIVE FULL STOP). The strings have the interesting property that their IDNA ToASCII output will contain embedded dots. For example:

```
ToASCII (hi U+248C com) = hi5.com
ToASCII (räksmörgås U+2024 com) = xn--rksmrgs.com-18as9u
```

This demonstrate the two general cases: The first where the ASCII dot is part of an output that do not begin with the IDN prefix xn--. The second example illustrate when the dot is part of IDN prefixed with xn--.

The input strings are, from the DNS point of view, a single label. The IDNA algorithm translate one label at a time. Thus, the output is expected to be only one label. What is important here is to make sure the DNS resolver receives the correct query. The DNS protocol does not use the dot to delimit labels on the wire, rather it uses length-value pairs. Thus the correct query would be for {7}hi5.com and {22}xn--rksmrgs.com-18as9u respectively.

Some implementations[1] have decided that these inputs strings are potentially confusing for the user. The string hi U+248C com looks like hi5.com on systems that support Unicode properly. These implementations do not follow RFC 3490. They yield:

```
ToASCII (hi U+248C com) = hi5.com
ToASCII (räksmörgås U+2024 com) = xn--rksmrgs-5wao1o.com
```

The DNS query they perform are {3}hi5{3}com and {18}xn--rksmrgs-5wao1o{3}com respectively. Arguably, this leads to a better user experience, and suggests that the IDNA specification is sub-optimal in this area.

B.1 Recommended Workaround

It has been suggested to normalize the entire input string using NFKC before passing it to IDNA ToASCII. You may use stringprep_utf8_nfkc_normalize or stringprep_ucs4_nfkc_normalize. This appears to lead to similar behaviour as IE/Firefox, which would avoid the problem, but this needs to be confirmed. Feel free to discuss the issue with us.

Alternative workarounds are being considered. Eventually Libidn may implement a new flag to the idna_* functions that implements a recommended way to work around this problem.

---

[1] Notably Microsoft's Internet Explorer and Mozilla's Firefox, but not Apple's Safari.

Appendix C Copying Information

C.1 GNU Free Documentation License

Version 1.3, 3 November 2008

Copyright © 2000, 2001, 2002, 2007, 2008 Free Software Foundation, Inc.
`http://fsf.org/`

0. PREAMBLE

   The purpose of this License is to make a manual, textbook, or other functional and useful document *free* in the sense of freedom: to assure everyone the effective freedom to copy and redistribute it, with or without modifying it, either commercially or non-commercially. Secondarily, this License preserves for the author and publisher a way to get credit for their work, while not being considered responsible for modifications made by others.

   This License is a kind of "copyleft", which means that derivative works of the document must themselves be free in the same sense. It complements the GNU General Public License, which is a copyleft license designed for free software.

   We have designed this License in order to use it for manuals for free software, because free software needs free documentation: a free program should come with manuals providing the same freedoms that the software does. But this License is not limited to software manuals; it can be used for any textual work, regardless of subject matter or whether it is published as a printed book. We recommend this License principally for works whose purpose is instruction or reference.

1. APPLICABILITY AND DEFINITIONS

   This License applies to any manual or other work, in any medium, that contains a notice placed by the copyright holder saying it can be distributed under the terms of this License. Such a notice grants a world-wide, royalty-free license, unlimited in duration, to use that work under the conditions stated herein. The "Document", below, refers to any such manual or work. Any member of the public is a licensee, and is addressed as "you". You accept the license if you copy, modify or distribute the work in a way requiring permission under copyright law.

   A "Modified Version" of the Document means any work containing the Document or a portion of it, either copied verbatim, or with modifications and/or translated into another language.

   A "Secondary Section" is a named appendix or a front-matter section of the Document that deals exclusively with the relationship of the publishers or authors of the Document to the Document's overall subject (or to related matters) and contains nothing that could fall directly within that overall subject. (Thus, if the Document is in part a textbook of mathematics, a Secondary Section may not explain any mathematics.) The relationship could be a matter of historical connection with the subject or with related matters, or of legal, commercial, philosophical, ethical or political position regarding them.

The "Invariant Sections" are certain Secondary Sections whose titles are designated, as being those of Invariant Sections, in the notice that says that the Document is released under this License. If a section does not fit the above definition of Secondary then it is not allowed to be designated as Invariant. The Document may contain zero Invariant Sections. If the Document does not identify any Invariant Sections then there are none.

The "Cover Texts" are certain short passages of text that are listed, as Front-Cover Texts or Back-Cover Texts, in the notice that says that the Document is released under this License. A Front-Cover Text may be at most 5 words, and a Back-Cover Text may be at most 25 words.

A "Transparent" copy of the Document means a machine-readable copy, represented in a format whose specification is available to the general public, that is suitable for revising the document straightforwardly with generic text editors or (for images composed of pixels) generic paint programs or (for drawings) some widely available drawing editor, and that is suitable for input to text formatters or for automatic translation to a variety of formats suitable for input to text formatters. A copy made in an otherwise Transparent file format whose markup, or absence of markup, has been arranged to thwart or discourage subsequent modification by readers is not Transparent. An image format is not Transparent if used for any substantial amount of text. A copy that is not "Transparent" is called "Opaque".

Examples of suitable formats for Transparent copies include plain ASCII without markup, Texinfo input format, LaTeX input format, SGML or XML using a publicly available DTD, and standard-conforming simple HTML, PostScript or PDF designed for human modification. Examples of transparent image formats include PNG, XCF and JPG. Opaque formats include proprietary formats that can be read and edited only by proprietary word processors, SGML or XML for which the DTD and/or processing tools are not generally available, and the machine-generated HTML, PostScript or PDF produced by some word processors for output purposes only.

The "Title Page" means, for a printed book, the title page itself, plus such following pages as are needed to hold, legibly, the material this License requires to appear in the title page. For works in formats which do not have any title page as such, "Title Page" means the text near the most prominent appearance of the work's title, preceding the beginning of the body of the text.

The "publisher" means any person or entity that distributes copies of the Document to the public.

A section "Entitled XYZ" means a named subunit of the Document whose title either is precisely XYZ or contains XYZ in parentheses following text that translates XYZ in another language. (Here XYZ stands for a specific section name mentioned below, such as "Acknowledgements", "Dedications", "Endorsements", or "History".) To "Preserve the Title" of such a section when you modify the Document means that it remains a section "Entitled XYZ" according to this definition.

The Document may include Warranty Disclaimers next to the notice which states that this License applies to the Document. These Warranty Disclaimers are considered to be included by reference in this License, but only as regards disclaiming warranties: any other implication that these Warranty Disclaimers may have is void and has no effect on the meaning of this License.

2. VERBATIM COPYING

You may copy and distribute the Document in any medium, either commercially or noncommercially, provided that this License, the copyright notices, and the license notice saying this License applies to the Document are reproduced in all copies, and that you add no other conditions whatsoever to those of this License. You may not use technical measures to obstruct or control the reading or further copying of the copies you make or distribute. However, you may accept compensation in exchange for copies. If you distribute a large enough number of copies you must also follow the conditions in section 3.

You may also lend copies, under the same conditions stated above, and you may publicly display copies.

3. COPYING IN QUANTITY

If you publish printed copies (or copies in media that commonly have printed covers) of the Document, numbering more than 100, and the Document's license notice requires Cover Texts, you must enclose the copies in covers that carry, clearly and legibly, all these Cover Texts: Front-Cover Texts on the front cover, and Back-Cover Texts on the back cover. Both covers must also clearly and legibly identify you as the publisher of these copies. The front cover must present the full title with all words of the title equally prominent and visible. You may add other material on the covers in addition. Copying with changes limited to the covers, as long as they preserve the title of the Document and satisfy these conditions, can be treated as verbatim copying in other respects.

If the required texts for either cover are too voluminous to fit legibly, you should put the first ones listed (as many as fit reasonably) on the actual cover, and continue the rest onto adjacent pages.

If you publish or distribute Opaque copies of the Document numbering more than 100, you must either include a machine-readable Transparent copy along with each Opaque copy, or state in or with each Opaque copy a computer-network location from which the general network-using public has access to download using public-standard network protocols a complete Transparent copy of the Document, free of added material. If you use the latter option, you must take reasonably prudent steps, when you begin distribution of Opaque copies in quantity, to ensure that this Transparent copy will remain thus accessible at the stated location until at least one year after the last time you distribute an Opaque copy (directly or through your agents or retailers) of that edition to the public.

It is requested, but not required, that you contact the authors of the Document well before redistributing any large number of copies, to give them a chance to provide you with an updated version of the Document.

4. MODIFICATIONS

You may copy and distribute a Modified Version of the Document under the conditions of sections 2 and 3 above, provided that you release the Modified Version under precisely this License, with the Modified Version filling the role of the Document, thus licensing distribution and modification of the Modified Version to whoever possesses a copy of it. In addition, you must do these things in the Modified Version:

A. Use in the Title Page (and on the covers, if any) a title distinct from that of the Document, and from those of previous versions (which should, if there were any, be listed in the History section of the Document). You may use the same title as a previous version if the original publisher of that version gives permission.

B. List on the Title Page, as authors, one or more persons or entities responsible for authorship of the modifications in the Modified Version, together with at least five of the principal authors of the Document (all of its principal authors, if it has fewer than five), unless they release you from this requirement.

C. State on the Title page the name of the publisher of the Modified Version, as the publisher.

D. Preserve all the copyright notices of the Document.

E. Add an appropriate copyright notice for your modifications adjacent to the other copyright notices.

F. Include, immediately after the copyright notices, a license notice giving the public permission to use the Modified Version under the terms of this License, in the form shown in the Addendum below.

G. Preserve in that license notice the full lists of Invariant Sections and required Cover Texts given in the Document's license notice.

H. Include an unaltered copy of this License.

I. Preserve the section Entitled "History", Preserve its Title, and add to it an item stating at least the title, year, new authors, and publisher of the Modified Version as given on the Title Page. If there is no section Entitled "History" in the Document, create one stating the title, year, authors, and publisher of the Document as given on its Title Page, then add an item describing the Modified Version as stated in the previous sentence.

J. Preserve the network location, if any, given in the Document for public access to a Transparent copy of the Document, and likewise the network locations given in the Document for previous versions it was based on. These may be placed in the "History" section. You may omit a network location for a work that was published at least four years before the Document itself, or if the original publisher of the version it refers to gives permission.

K. For any section Entitled "Acknowledgements" or "Dedications", Preserve the Title of the section, and preserve in the section all the substance and tone of each of the contributor acknowledgements and/or dedications given therein.

L. Preserve all the Invariant Sections of the Document, unaltered in their text and in their titles. Section numbers or the equivalent are not considered part of the section titles.

M. Delete any section Entitled "Endorsements". Such a section may not be included in the Modified Version.

N. Do not retitle any existing section to be Entitled "Endorsements" or to conflict in title with any Invariant Section.

O. Preserve any Warranty Disclaimers.

If the Modified Version includes new front-matter sections or appendices that qualify as Secondary Sections and contain no material copied from the Document, you may at your option designate some or all of these sections as invariant. To do this, add their titles to the list of Invariant Sections in the Modified Version's license notice. These titles must be distinct from any other section titles.

You may add a section Entitled "Endorsements", provided it contains nothing but endorsements of your Modified Version by various parties—for example, statements of peer review or that the text has been approved by an organization as the authoritative definition of a standard.

You may add a passage of up to five words as a Front-Cover Text, and a passage of up to 25 words as a Back-Cover Text, to the end of the list of Cover Texts in the Modified Version. Only one passage of Front-Cover Text and one of Back-Cover Text may be added by (or through arrangements made by) any one entity. If the Document already includes a cover text for the same cover, previously added by you or by arrangement made by the same entity you are acting on behalf of, you may not add another; but you may replace the old one, on explicit permission from the previous publisher that added the old one.

The author(s) and publisher(s) of the Document do not by this License give permission to use their names for publicity for or to assert or imply endorsement of any Modified Version.

5. COMBINING DOCUMENTS

You may combine the Document with other documents released under this License, under the terms defined in section 4 above for modified versions, provided that you include in the combination all of the Invariant Sections of all of the original documents, unmodified, and list them all as Invariant Sections of your combined work in its license notice, and that you preserve all their Warranty Disclaimers.

The combined work need only contain one copy of this License, and multiple identical Invariant Sections may be replaced with a single copy. If there are multiple Invariant Sections with the same name but different contents, make the title of each such section unique by adding at the end of it, in parentheses, the name of the original author or publisher of that section if known, or else a unique number. Make the same adjustment to the section titles in the list of Invariant Sections in the license notice of the combined work.

In the combination, you must combine any sections Entitled "History" in the various original documents, forming one section Entitled "History"; likewise combine any sections Entitled "Acknowledgements", and any sections Entitled "Dedications". You must delete all sections Entitled "Endorsements."

6. COLLECTIONS OF DOCUMENTS

You may make a collection consisting of the Document and other documents released under this License, and replace the individual copies of this License in the various documents with a single copy that is included in the collection, provided that you follow the rules of this License for verbatim copying of each of the documents in all other respects.

You may extract a single document from such a collection, and distribute it individually under this License, provided you insert a copy of this License into the extracted document, and follow this License in all other respects regarding verbatim copying of that document.

7. AGGREGATION WITH INDEPENDENT WORKS

A compilation of the Document or its derivatives with other separate and independent documents or works, in or on a volume of a storage or distribution medium, is called an "aggregate" if the copyright resulting from the compilation is not used to limit the legal rights of the compilation's users beyond what the individual works permit. When the Document is included in an aggregate, this License does not apply to the other works in the aggregate which are not themselves derivative works of the Document.

If the Cover Text requirement of section 3 is applicable to these copies of the Document, then if the Document is less than one half of the entire aggregate, the Document's Cover Texts may be placed on covers that bracket the Document within the aggregate, or the electronic equivalent of covers if the Document is in electronic form. Otherwise they must appear on printed covers that bracket the whole aggregate.

8. TRANSLATION

Translation is considered a kind of modification, so you may distribute translations of the Document under the terms of section 4. Replacing Invariant Sections with translations requires special permission from their copyright holders, but you may include translations of some or all Invariant Sections in addition to the original versions of these Invariant Sections. You may include a translation of this License, and all the license notices in the Document, and any Warranty Disclaimers, provided that you also include the original English version of this License and the original versions of those notices and disclaimers. In case of a disagreement between the translation and the original version of this License or a notice or disclaimer, the original version will prevail.

If a section in the Document is Entitled "Acknowledgements", "Dedications", or "History", the requirement (section 4) to Preserve its Title (section 1) will typically require changing the actual title.

9. TERMINATION

You may not copy, modify, sublicense, or distribute the Document except as expressly provided under this License. Any attempt otherwise to copy, modify, sublicense, or distribute it is void, and will automatically terminate your rights under this License.

However, if you cease all violation of this License, then your license from a particular copyright holder is reinstated (a) provisionally, unless and until the copyright holder explicitly and finally terminates your license, and (b) permanently, if the copyright holder fails to notify you of the violation by some reasonable means prior to 60 days after the cessation.

Moreover, your license from a particular copyright holder is reinstated permanently if the copyright holder notifies you of the violation by some reasonable means, this is the first time you have received notice of violation of this License (for any work) from that copyright holder, and you cure the violation prior to 30 days after your receipt of the notice.

Termination of your rights under this section does not terminate the licenses of parties who have received copies or rights from you under this License. If your rights have been terminated and not permanently reinstated, receipt of a copy of some or all of the same material does not give you any rights to use it.

10. FUTURE REVISIONS OF THIS LICENSE

The Free Software Foundation may publish new, revised versions of the GNU Free Documentation License from time to time. Such new versions will be similar in spirit to the present version, but may differ in detail to address new problems or concerns. See http://www.gnu.org/copyleft/.

Each version of the License is given a distinguishing version number. If the Document specifies that a particular numbered version of this License "or any later version" applies to it, you have the option of following the terms and conditions either of that specified version or of any later version that has been published (not as a draft) by the Free Software Foundation. If the Document does not specify a version number of this License, you may choose any version ever published (not as a draft) by the Free Software Foundation. If the Document specifies that a proxy can decide which future versions of this License can be used, that proxy's public statement of acceptance of a version permanently authorizes you to choose that version for the Document.

11. RELICENSING

"Massive Multiauthor Collaboration Site" (or "MMC Site") means any World Wide Web server that publishes copyrightable works and also provides prominent facilities for anybody to edit those works. A public wiki that anybody can edit is an example of such a server. A "Massive Multiauthor Collaboration" (or "MMC") contained in the site means any set of copyrightable works thus published on the MMC site.

"CC-BY-SA" means the Creative Commons Attribution-Share Alike 3.0 license published by Creative Commons Corporation, a not-for-profit corporation with a principal place of business in San Francisco, California, as well as future copyleft versions of that license published by that same organization.

"Incorporate" means to publish or republish a Document, in whole or in part, as part of another Document.

An MMC is "eligible for relicensing" if it is licensed under this License, and if all works that were first published under this License somewhere other than this MMC, and subsequently incorporated in whole or in part into the MMC, (1) had no cover texts or invariant sections, and (2) were thus incorporated prior to November 1, 2008.

The operator of an MMC Site may republish an MMC contained in the site under CC-BY-SA on the same site at any time before August 1, 2009, provided the MMC is eligible for relicensing.

ADDENDUM: How to use this License for your documents

To use this License in a document you have written, include a copy of the License in the document and put the following copyright and license notices just after the title page:

```
Copyright (C)  year  your name.
Permission is granted to copy, distribute and/or modify this document
under the terms of the GNU Free Documentation License, Version 1.3
or any later version published by the Free Software Foundation;
with no Invariant Sections, no Front-Cover Texts, and no Back-Cover
Texts.  A copy of the license is included in the section entitled ``GNU
Free Documentation License''.
```

If you have Invariant Sections, Front-Cover Texts and Back-Cover Texts, replace the "with...Texts." line with this:

```
with the Invariant Sections being list their titles, with
the Front-Cover Texts being list, and with the Back-Cover Texts
being list.
```

If you have Invariant Sections without Cover Texts, or some other combination of the three, merge those two alternatives to suit the situation.

If your document contains nontrivial examples of program code, we recommend releasing these examples in parallel under your choice of free software license, such as the GNU General Public License, to permit their use in free software.

Function and Variable Index

Concept Index